EDUCATIONAL REFORM IN POST PANDEMIC SITUATION

RECOVERY AND STRENGTHENING OF EDUCATION

DR. PANKAJ KUMAR PAUL & SIBNATH MANNA

Dedicated To

Dr. Chitralekha Mehera, Associate Professor, Department of Education, The University of Burdwan.

For her guidance, constructive criticism and inspiring help which enable us completed this edited Book.

Review committee

Dr. Dulal Mukhopadhyay	Ex-prof, Department of Education, University of Kalyani.
Dr. Tarak Kumar Pan	Ex-prof, Bidya Bhabana, Visva Bharati
Dr. Chitralekha Mehera	Associate Professor, Department of Education, The University of Burdwan, Burdwan
Dr. Rajiba Lochan Mohapatra	Assistant Professor, Department of Education, The University of Burdwan, b Burdwan
Dr. Puja Sarkar (Bal)	Assistant Professor, Department of Education, The University of Burdwan, Burdwan

Contents

Foreword

Educational institutions in India were based mostly on traditional methods of learning. They are following traditional the face-to-face lectures in a classroom. But Covid-19 has changed the total educational scenario. Online teaching-learning has taken a big position over lightly. The whole education system across the world faced a challenge and forced to shift to online mode of teaching-learning. They had no options but to shift the system to online entirely. The deadly Corona Virus has deeply affected the global economy which has shaken up the educational sector also. There was a great fear of loosing outgoing semester and even more in the coming future. Gradually it became uncertain to get back to normal education system anytime soon. Educational Institutions were straggling to find the options to deal with the disaster. An urgent need to protect and save our nation, especially our education came up. Several arguments associated with different processes of teaching-learning pedagogy had taken place. Online mode teaching-learning were accepted to be a relatively chapter based on accessibility.

The present book is the outcome of concerns about the options to deal with disaster after post Covid-19 shutdown and provide a basis reference tool for researchers and academics.

Dr. Chitralekha Mehera
Assiociate Professor
The University of Burdwan

Preface

Covid-19 has already started changing various aspects nationally and globally and one such aspect is the Educational sector. The present edited book entitled "Educational Reform in Post Pandemic Situation." is an attempt to contribute in the field of education as well as different aspects of recovering and strengthening in the context of Indian Education. The three broad objectives of education are the grant of knowledge, imparting skill sets to increase employability and inculcation of values and ideals so that student can perform a constructive role in shaping the progressive modern society. In order to achieve these objectives, the Indian education system as an ecosystem must function organically in tandem with its main components viz; the students, the parents, society and the educational institutions. The efficiency of the educational ecosystem is adversely affected by the outbreak of COVID-19 pandemic situation. Various academic activities at all levels of the education system were adjourned sine die. The present scenario has jeopardized the educational ecosystem to achieve its objectives. In this regard, multifront reforms are needed for the efficient functioning of the education system in the post-COVID-19 situation. We can turn the challenges posed by the pandemic into opportunities, beyond the present crisis, and can enhance the overall efficiency of our education system.

This book is edited and written in simple and lucid style. The presentation of various topics of this book has been made research centered and researcher oriented. It is hoped that this book proves to be very useful resource for all concern and is expected to be a trustworthy to researchers and students in every field of education.

We shall feel amply rewarded if it arouses a genuine interest among the researchers and students of education.

Burdwan, 2022

Dr. Pankaj Kumar Paul
Sibnath Manna

Acknowledgements

We are pleased to acknowledge our indebtedness to all the authors for their scholarly contribution in completing this book. Our sincere thanks and deep appreciation go to all the reviewers who spend their valuable time in this regard. We also take this opportunity to express our sincere thanks to all those persons whose valuable advice enriched us in connection with this work. We wish to express our appreciation to Notion Press for undertaking this publication work in a meticulous manner.

Dr. Pankaj Kumar Paul
Sibnath Manna

Prologue

COVID-19 has posed serious challenges to the progress of education around the world. We have faced an unprecedented experience in our life. Education is no exception. Among the diverse experiences from different institutions and instructors, conversely, there was a common thread: how to meet learning outcomes and achieve student success despite sudden and radical changes in our lives and those of our students. The pandemic situation of COVID-19 makes it easier for us to think about how to take initiatives to rethink education and how knowledge and education can shape the future of humanity and the planet. COVID-19 has brought dangerous times for education, with the risk of fragmentation and unraveling as we lose both teachers and students who may not be able to return once they return to school. Nevertheless, we also have to admit that many parents and communities have woken up to praise the work of teachers and their professionalism. More and more people are becoming aware of the multiple roles that schools play in ensuring the health and nutrition of children and youth in addition to academic learning. This increased awareness and appreciation can serve as the basis for a new revival of public education. The pandemic has forced a massive shift from learning and teaching to traditional settings with physical interaction. This is a major problem for children living in poverty worldwide, who often depend on the physical setting of their schools for learning materials, guidance and, sometimes, the only proper meal of the day.

The present book is a contribution to deal about the new methods of teaching and learning to the context of post-COVID situation. It consists of various views of educationists, academicians and scholars on the restoration of education and strengthening of education in the light of the post-COVID pandemic situation which helps us to know the ways of renewal of education, human interaction and well-being of human society that should be given topmost priority. In these circumstances we have become accustomed to digitally based technologies that enable communication, collaboration and learning across distances – a powerful tool, not a panacea but a source of innovation and expanded possibilities. To protect the right to education in the extraordinary circumstances created by the pandemic, and to facilitate the level of trust necessary for global co-operation to mobilize resources to support the universal right to education, we call on all education stakeholders to monitor the use of educational resources in a optimum and feasible manner to safeguard entitlements and capabilities of learners.

CHAPTER ONE

EDUCATION: A FOOD FOR OUR MIND AND A DRINK FOR OUR HEART

Rajiba Lochan Mohapatra, Ph.D.

Assistant Professor, Department of Education, The University of Burdwan

PROLOGUE: Nothing can stop an idea whose time has come– this famous quote of Victor Hugo is apt in the present context of education. Education, whose only intention has so far been that of a job provider, has not always been the same. The octopus of 'consumerism' has entrapped it and made it a synonym of job. But the idea *'sikshya'* or *'vidya'* is not providing job, but enriching the learner from every side. From a comprehensive education we have come to a stage where education means getting a job after passing out a particular course. But the problem of this education is that it failed to teach the life skills essential for smooth survival. So even if one gets a job s/he faces multiple problems relating to life. Our education system does not touch this aspect. So far we have neglected it deliberately, but the pandemic has brought it to the limelight. After millions of lives lost and homes dilapidated, humanity is trying hard to decipher why it suffered the way it suffered. The answer is 'we have deranged from the path we are supposed to take' and therefore suffered. We have gone to the far end of consumerism for which nature gave a clarion call of *'Traahi Maam'*. And we have no other way but to listen to her. And we are listening to her. We now start listening to the ideas that are perennial and eternal. We now are thinking to change the pattern of our life style. The global healthcare system is undergoing a massive change to make itself fit to the neo-normal. Recently, we have brought a new system of education known as NEP-2020. But a sorry state of affair is that we are doing these actions after paying a huge cost, i.e., huge loss of life and massive waste of wealth.

EDUCATION: A FOOD FOR THE MIND

Taitiriya Upanishad tells about five sheaths of a human being known as 'kosa'. The first one is 'annamaya kosa' meaning the sheath that is maintained by 'anna' or food. We can call it– the physical being. The survival of this very being is completely dependent on food. Otherwise one can die. Likewise, the next sheath or 'kosa' is 'pranamaya kosa' or the vital being. Its survival depends on the physical activities and exercises. The third sheath or 'kosa' is called 'manomaya kosa' or the mental being. Its survival depends on proper education and training of the mind and emotions. Similarly, the fourth and fifth layers are 'vijnanamaya kosa' or psychic being and 'anandamaya kosa' or the spiritual being respectively. Their nurturing happens when higher form of meditations is practiced. But, as of now, let's focus on the third layer, the mental being. This is because the development of this sheath is directly related to education.

A true education of the mind, that prepares man for a higher life, has five phases. Usually these phases follow one after another, but for some exceptional individuals they may change the order or even proceed simultaneously. These five phases are:

(1) Development of the power of concentration, the capacity of attention.

(2) Development of the capacities of expansion, widening, complexity and richness.

(3) Development of the capacity to organise one's ideas around a central idea, a higher ideal or a supremely luminous idea that will serve as a guiding light in life.

(4) Thought-control, rejection of unwanted thoughts, ability to think what one wants to think and when one wants to think.

(5) Development of mental silence, absolute tranquility and a total receptivity to inspirations coming from the higher regions of the being.

But if we observe the present education system, it does very little for the training of mind. The pandemic has taught hard lessons of life. During this time, physical activity was reduced to minimum. There were no social gatherings. Stress was on mental activity. As people were not trained mentally, they experienced all kinds of psychological traumas and troubles. They failed to control their inner demon and fell flat. The pandemic has more fully roused the basic problem that education has so far neglected. Now, it is our duty to concentrate on these aspects and revive education to its full. Let's concentrate how we can do it.

Firstly, every system of education, beginning from primary to higher, must have to include 'pranayama' and meditation as a compulsory part of the curriculum. These two are the sure sought approach for complete mental control and rejuvenation. Every day, at least one routine period must be devoted to this activity. There must be a hall or big room well equipped for this. And if there is open space it is better. But meditation in open space is not always feasible. Because meditation during rain, in scorching heat and in extreme cold is not practicable in open. Therefore, it is better to have an all weather hall that can accommodate large number of students for this purpose. A regular teacher or trainer must be appointed for this purpose.

Secondly, students are to be advised to observe silence beyond school or college hours. As the physical body requires rest so does the mind. Silence gives rest to the mind. The art of resting one's mind is something to be acquired. Changing one's mental activity is surely a way of resting; but the greatest possible rest is silence. A few minutes of observed calmness are better than hour long sleep. This observance of silence will make the learner more creative, help him/her become a great problem solver, and improves his/her concentration to the maximum.

Thirdly, the teachers in their respective subjects should as far as practicable give tasks of non-conventional and brain-storming type. This would help the learners think and innovate. Scientific studies have proven the fact that ninety five percent of an average human brain remains unused. And our system of education has nothing to do to activate this unused vast. To make that large chunk active, we must give problems and exercises that would galvanize the brain cells and make them active. This would open the floodgates of knowledge and innovation for us. All scientific and technological innovations, philosophical inquiries have been because the mind somehow touched the vast. For most scientists and philosophers this touching of the unconscious vast is occasional and unmethodical. But, we can make this happen methodical through proper education. Creative ways of teaching and interacting with the students can make it happen.

EDUCATION: A DRINK FOR THE HEART

If we analyse the taxonomy of objectives in education, we will find a domain called the affective domain. This domain gives importance to emotion, sentiment, feeling and a lot more related things. A significant part of our life is at mess because we have never trained these faculties in schools and colleges. Now that the time demands, we are talking about it. But the question is how to train this affective faculty so that things happen in our life as smooth and moderated as possible? It is said that when our heart blossoms, our perception becomes holistic. For a flower to blossom, required amount of water and other nutrients are needed. If it does not get that, its full blooming is halted. Likewise, to make every individual heart blossom, right kind of education is to be provided. In the language of modern education this is called 360 degree education. To bring this completion, education should be holistic. Now the question comes, what is holistic education? Defining 'holistic education', the first National Holistic Education Conference of USA (1979) states:

Holistic Education

- (a) "Recognizes that human beings seek meaning, not just fact or skills, as an intrinsic aspect of their full and healthy development."
- (b) "Is not one particular curriculum or methodology; it is a set of working assumptions"
- (c) is based on "a dynamic, open human relationship."
- (d) "Cultivates a critical awareness of the many contexts of learners' lives - moral, cultural, ecological, economic, technological, and political."
- (e) Perceives that "All persons hold vast multi-faceted potentials" and "Human intelligence is expressed through diverse styles and capacities"
- (f) believes that the thinking process is "contextual, intuitive, creative, and physical ways of knowing."
- (g) accepts that learning is a "lifelong process;" takes cognizance of all life situations" and is both an inner process of self-discovery and a cooperative activity
- (h) is "active, self-motivated, supportive, and encouraging of the human spirit."
- (i) considers the curriculum as "interdisciplinary, integrating both community and global perspectives."

NEP 2020 says, "A holistic and multi-disciplinary education would aim to develop all capacities of human beings -intellectual, aesthetic, social, physical, emotional, and moral in an integrated manner."

In India we find example of holistic education from the ancient time. (MHRD 2020, pp.36-38) speaks about Banabhatta's "Kadambari" that envisages good education as knowledge about the sixty-four *kalaas* or arts. Students were taught four aspects of education: *swadharma, samaja dharma, rastra dharma* and *viswa dharma*. It was considered heartless, if the learner, after completing education, only concentrated on self development (swadharma). True students need to make balance of these four *dharmas*. Ancient Gurus also adhered to these four *dharmas*. They were also found to be excellent all-rounders. From highest philosophical discourse to agriculture and archery, it seemed they mastered almost every discipline. Because of that people were leading a life of ease and happiness. Education based on dharma can bring perennial happiness for all. And if we deviate from it, problem mounts in our life. In Mahabharata, Vidura advises Dhrutarastra, to abandon his son Duryodhana, even if he (Duryodhana) is his own. In this context Vidura says,

tyajed ekam kulasyarthe gramasyarthe kulam tyajet I
gramam janapadasyarthe atmarthe prthivim tyajet II

[That is, "for protecting a family, one person may be abandoned; for protecting a village, a family may be abandoned; for the protection of society, a town may be abandoned; and for the protection of the Atman, even the earth may be abandoned"].

What Vidura wanted to tell to Dhrutarastra was to follow the *Samaja Dharma*. A mere education of mind may make you shrewd and cruelly selfish. In Mahabharata, Duryodhana was the greatest example. In modern times, terrorists and persons who commit cyber crimes are people with higher mental faculty but with no hearts. The difference between APJ Abdul Kalam and Osama Bin Laden is not of mind but of heart. Both had excellent mental capabilities; but the former was highly constructive while the later was found destructive. So, it is education of the heart that matters even more. But the question is how can we provide this systematically through education? Let's discuss it.

Ron Miller (2000) has talked about five levels of wholeness. Our education system must see whether these five levels are achieved or not. These are–the whole person, the whole community, the whole society, the whole planet and the whole cosmos. The system in general and curriculum in particular must ensure wholeness at these five levels. The first level demands that a person must be viewed as an integration of six elements: physical, emotional, intellectual, social, aesthetic, and spiritual. And education must reflect all these elements as needed to exist meaningfully. The second level talks about quality human relationship. Through our numerous interactions we must try to establish healthy and meaningful relationship with others. Education should have a deliberate attempt to help the learners knowing the art of establishing relationship with other community members. The third level wants every learner to understand social crises and prevailing situations and accordingly act for establishing order in society. The fourth level intends the learner to know about the systems and sub-systems working to make the planet peaceful. Some of these systems are the political system, the economic system, the environmental system etc. These systems have their sub-systems. Any problem in any of these systems would result in the destruction of this beautiful planet. For example, the world is experiencing a massive environmental degradation. The learners must be trained to think in this direction and have necessary awareness about the crises that the world is facing. The last level says about the values like universal love, compassion, peace, brotherhood which makes the cosmos running. The Vedas call it 'ritah' or the cosmic force of balance. This would give meaning to the life we lead on earth. The learners must know in their learning system these cosmic values and how they impact our lives.

UNESCO (1996) in its report "Learning the Treasure Within" speaks about the four pillars of learning–learning to learn, learning to do, learning to live together and learning to be. We need to model our education in this direction. The first dimension speaks about developing consciousness in the search of knowledge which includes attributes like paying attention, listening, perceiving, and developing curiosity, intuitiveness, and creativity. However, this never speaks about rote learning. Learners need to be oriented in such a way that they develop faculties like this. This would not only help them in understanding but also in creating knowledge for themselves and for others. The second aspect tells about "learning to adapt to the needs of work and ability to work in a team, along with the strategic use of knowledge to resolve problems and make rational decisions in generating quality goods and services. Learning to do means knowing how to take risks as well as take the initiative"(Schreiner, 2005). Importance is given on application of knowledge in present life situation. The third pillar says about living a life of dignity, respect to others, and co-operation with others. To live peacefully, one must abandon the dogmas and prejudices and go beyond fissiparous tendencies. Education must help the learners generate the essential values of healthful living. The fourth pillar is about discovering one's self and its relationship with the whole of humanity. . "It is learning to belong to the whole. It is the discovery of our universal dimension, where genuine human values, not individual human values, reside. It is the discovery of one's own being and the inner wisdom achieved through self knowledge. Holistic education nurtures this learning in a special way, by recognizing the human being as a basically spiritual being in search of meaning" (Nava, 2001). " 'Learning to be' therefore is to be interpreted as learning to be human, through acquisition of knowledge, skills and values conducive to personality development in its intellectual, moral, cultural and physical dimensions. This implies a curriculum aiming at cultivating qualities of imagination and creativity; acquiring universally shared human values; developing aspects of a person's potential: memory, reasoning, aesthetic sense, physical capacity and communication/social skills; developing critical thinking and exercising independent judgment; and developing personal commitment and responsibility" (Schreiner, 2005).

EPILOGUE:

Education for the mind and for the heart requires education that encompasses every activity that a learner may need to perform in order to be a quality citizen not only of one's country but also for the whole world. A corrupt education system would bring collapse to the whole society, or even to the whole nation. The pandemic, the Russia-Ukraine war, terrorism in Africa, Middle-East and other parts of the world have amply proven the need of a healthy and meaningful education. To make the system robust and comprehensive UNESCO (1996)'s suggestion is to be strictly adopted by the system of education. Sri Aurobindo speaks about Integral Education which encompasses education of the five sheaths as discussed above. Necessary change in Curriculum, organization of Managerial system, and sufficient orientation of the teaching community are some of the basic steps required to make things happen for a better tomorrow.

REFERENCES

MHRD (2020) *National Education Policy 2020*, Govt. f India, New Delhi.

Miller, J. P. (2019a) Preface. In Miller, J. P., Nigh, K., Binder, M.J., Novak, B., & Crowel, S.

(Eds.), *International Handbook of Holistic Education* (pp.xxiii-xxv). Routledge, New York.

Mohanty, S.B. (2021) Holistic education: a vital recommendation of national education policy – 2020,

University News 59, 45, 17-21,November 08-14.

Miller, R. (2000). Caring for new life: Essays on holistic education. Brandon, VT: Foundation for Educational Renewal.

Mahmoudi, S., Jafari, E.,Nasrabadi, H.A.,Liaghatdar, M.J.(2012). Holistic Education: An Approach for 21 Century, In *International Education Studies, Vol.* 5, No. 2; April 2012

https://files.eric.ed.gov/fulltext/EJ1066819.pdf

Nava, R, G. (2001). Holistic education: Pedagogy of universal love. Brandon: Holistic education press.

Schreiner, P., Banev, S., & Oxly,S. (2005). Holistic education Resource Book, Verlage: Waxmann.

WEBLINK

http://www.sriaurobindoinstitute.org/saioc/educational/ integral_education/mental_education#mental

CHAPTER TWO

Blended Learning in Post-Pandemic India: Revamping Higher Education

Dr. Tulika Chakraborty

Assistant Professor in Education, Domkal Girls' College, Murshidabad, WB, India

Abstract

The world has been devastated by the COVID-19 epidemic. On March 11, 2020, the World Health Organization (WHO) announced it a Pandemic. It has interrupted education in more than 150 countries, affecting approximately 1.6 billion students. During in the initial stage of COVID-19, the education response focused on establishing remote learning as just a rapid response. This was intended to reach out to all students, but they were not always successful. Education system is now available in the majority of countries, either partially or fully. In this day and age, blended learning has the potential to meet more of the academic needs of learners. During this time, schools around the world are revamping their academic systems to be more blended, and blended learning has become the new reality in the post-pandemic era. Blended learning (BL) is addition of traditional face-to-face and online instruction. BL use face-to-face instruction techniques such as direct instruction or lecture, discussion groups, and small-group work while also using new tech needed in online learning so pupils can do their academic work at home if they have access to this necessary technology. Because of the use of information and communications technologies (ICTs), the entire teaching pedagogy has been transformed into learner-centered pedagogy. Throughout this period, teachers who never instructed an online class, and perhaps hardly used technology in their own classroom with their students had to seek about using BL and put their initiative into assigned tasks, activities, practical etc. So, in this post-pandemic scenario, BL can enable learners who are introverted and shy to share their knowledge and thoughts from others by using group discussions where conversations that began at school can continue long after this pandemic has over.

Keywords: *Blended Learning (BL), Pedagogy, Post-pandemic, ICT, IPSIT*

Introduction

During the pandemic outbreak of COVID-19, the world is rapidly changing, as well as the numerous domains are also being influenced by this transformation. The advancement of digital learning technologies has had a massive impact on educational institutions, eventually pushing traditional methods to the sidelines. In the post-pandemic era, both technique and traditional teaching and learning methods are critical. As a result, the Blended Learning (BL) system combines the art of virtual learning tools with the more traditional classrooms with face-to-face teaching. BL could be the answer to providing education in the post-pandemic era of 21st century India. Actually, the post-pandemic era begin after the impact of the Covid-19. Actually, the post-pandemic era begin after the influence of the Covid-19. BL does not simply refer to a combination of online and face-to-face modes; rather, it relates to the well combination of important activities in both modes. BL is the concern of several factors, the most important factors are learning outcomes and student instructional environment. Given the emergence of digital technologies, as well as the increased significance of technology for teaching-learning at the lowest levels from school to higher educational institution, the NEP 2020 suggested the use of BL mode. Because of the current pandemic scenario, the NEP-2020 suggests promoting online technology in education, while emphasizing the significance of face-to-face in-person learning.

Objectives of the study

The objectives of the study are as follows-

1. To discuss the important features and benefits of BL and the role of teacher & Student in it

during the Post Pandemic period.

2. To understand ICT initiatives of BL and discuss the method of implementation of BL during

the Post-Covid situation.

3. To analyse some innovative trends in Evaluation & Assessment of BL during the Post-Covid

period and also propose some measures of BL for the improvement of entire education system.

i. **The important features and benefits of BL in Post-Covid situation**

BL is an effective learning procedure all across India during and after a crisis. Technology-enabled BL allows for learning at any time and from any location, allowing students to learn without the constraints of time and place, but with the potential support of teacher engagement.

Some important features and benefits of BL are as follows:

• Increase pupil involvement in the learning process,

• Improve teaching - learning process interaction, increasing responsibility for learning,

• Enhance time - management skills and support system, improve overall student learning

outcomes,

• Improve institutional reputation,

• Establish more adaptable classroom atmosphere, helping more conducive to self and learning,

• Increase the opportunity for experiential education.

The following are some of the key benefits of BL:

• <u>Increased flexibility</u>: BL makes the learning resources and experiences more flexible,

dependable, reliable, and reproducible.

• <u>Increases interaction</u>: BL provided a platform for greater interactivity between students and teachers.

• <u>Improved learning</u>: More types of learning activities increase engagement and may allows learners achieve higher and more purposeful levels of learning.

• <u>Learning to be virtual people</u>: Digital learning skills are now necessary to be a lifelong learner, and blended courses assist students in using a lot of skills and techniques.

v. **The role of teachers and students in BL in the aftermath of a pandemic**

• **Teachers' Role in BL**

BL transforms the teacher's role from that of a knowledge provider to that of an educator and mentor. This shift does not imply that teachers are no longer involved in their students' education. Teachers had a superb impact on students' learning during in the Post Pandemic scenario. Classroom instruction has traditionally been largely teacher-directed, but even in BL, it is becoming more student-centered. BL strikes an optimal balance among online instructions that offer interactive, technology-based acquiring knowledge, individualised pacing, and privacy, all of which keep students engaged and motivated.

BL results in more frequent and individual teacher engagement with individual students, giving teachers the opportunity to deepen and enhance student-teacher relationship. So, in this post-pandemic situation, BL integrates the most basic features of digital learning with the most effective aspects of specific instructions, allowing teachers to do far more to meet the needs of their students without adding to their already heavy workload.

• **The Learner's Role in BL**

1. **Enhance students' interests**: Once the technology is integrated in to the school lessons, students are more likely to be interested in, concentrated on, and enthused about the topics being studied.

2. **Maintain students focused for prolonged learning**: Using computers and the internet to engage and interact with resources can help students concentrate for longer periods of time.

3. **Improves student independence**: The use of e-learning materials improves a student's capacity to track appropriate learning objectives and assist his or her peers.

4. **Increases the stability**: Students are becoming stable, self-driven and responsible, trying to track their accomplishments, which helps them to develop the flexibility to strive out resources and become self-advocates in order to achieve their goals.

5. **Encourage student ownership**: BL instills a sense of 'student ownership over learning,' which could be a powerful force propelling education. This responsibility contributes to the sensation of ownership.

6. **Allow for instant diagnostics and learning outcome**: The ability to quickly analyse, review, and provide feedback on student work gives

teachers the ability to customize his teaching method and feedback to each student while working to improve time efficiency. If necessary, an instructor or teacher can help accelerate the education system or provide more advanced resources.

v. BL's ICT initiatives in the aftermath of a pandemic

Teachers are now assisting students in managing various learning situations in the post-pandemic period. It is the responsibility of teachers and learning developers to provide blended activities that better suits the topic, the needs of the learners, and the curriculum requirements.

BL's ICT initiatives include the following:

• <u>MOOCs</u>: A MOOC is a web-based education system that offers a variety of courses with the goal of encouraging massive internet interactive participation as well as open access. MOOCs aim provide the real-time education online by utilising 13 various characteristics such as media content, educational resources, questionnaires, online exams, and so on.

• <u>SWAYAM</u>: SWAYAM is a programme launched by the GOI with the vision of attaining the three basic principles of education policy: access, equity, and quality. The aim of this effort is to provide all disadvantaged students with more basic teaching-learning resources.

•<u>SimLab+</u>: SimLab+ has the potential to be a process-oriented, multidisciplinary simulation environment for accurately analysing the performance of complex assemblies. SimLab+ is intended to be a powerful 3D visualisation as well as a communication platform with a stylish set of built-in workbenches.

•<u>Virtual Lab</u>: A virtual lab allows for remote connectivity to labs in all major scientific and engineering disciplines. These Digital Labs can assist undergraduate and graduate students, and also research scholars.

• <u>Robotics</u>: Robotics is a branch of science that includes degree in electrical engineering, applied research, and many other disciplines. Educational institutions are in charge of the making plans, construction, and application of robotic systems, sensory systems, and knowledge processing.

•**FOSSEE**: FOSSEE (Free/Libre and Open Source Software for Education) program encourages the work opportunities of educational tools in academic and research.

• **SBHS**: The single-board heater system (SBHS) will be used as a lab-in-a-box for teaching and learning control systems.

- **Blogging**: The teacher creates a blog, and students are invited to contribute to it. A issue, idea, or actual problem could be provided with the some resource base to the learners' points of view, concepts, opinions, explanations, scenarios, and so on, and they will be asked to join to contribute to the blog.

• **Sticky notes**: Online brainstorming can be done with sticky note techniques such as IdeaFlip, Lino.it, Jamboard, and others. An online assessment, brainstormed ideas is usually performed as a synchronous task in an exceedingly live online class. This type of generating ideas is commonly referred to it as an asynchronous activity.

• **Shared documents**: In small team like, 2 to 5 students were asked to directly introduce some tools like google Docs, Google Sheets, Etherpad, ScatterSpoke, IdeaBoard, and others. Most of the other tools are available, and students could use them when they want as long since they have internet access.

• **Concept-mapping, Mindmapping, and Infographic Tools**: Cooperative learning, Concept-mapping and Mindmapping ICT techniques such as Miro, Google Drawing, Conceptboard, Coggle, Bubble.us, and the others assist online learners in discussing and developing relationships of issues connected with a subject matter.

• **Comprehensive activity platforms**: Comprehensive activity platforms such as Padlet, Miro, Whimsical, and others may prove useful as virtual workspaces. Features such as wireframes will help learners develop project management and teamwork skills, which are essential for 21st century learners.

v. **The process of implementing BL in a post-pandemic situation**

Implementing BL in the post-pandemic period necessitates a science based, planned instructional process. A effective instructional process must combine appropriate pedagogies such as BL with appropriate technologies.

The BL implementation process is detailed below.

• Coming up with ideas

In higher education, learners are mature and experience. They already have prior knowledge from school and previous years of education. They generate new ideas for additional data sources. Learners may be able to take advantage of this opportunity if they use BL mode. Before classroom sessions, resources will be uploaded and external links may be published on Learning Management Systems.

Brainstorming

Brainstorming exercises always help learners think more spontaneously, derive solutions and ideas, appreciate others' concepts, and take delight in the creation from several ideas by the group members instead of listening to only the teachers' ideas and views. It fosters a sense of responsibility to believe about and learn about oneself.

• Mind-mapping/Concept-mapping

The best conceptual exercise for learners is to create the conceptual framework of any subject within their minds. These assist learners in understanding the issue from all angles and in determining relationships between ideas on their own.

• Ingenious Presentations

Learning, at any level and in any subject, should help students develop their abilities. Infographics, short videos, and podcasts allow them to present their knowledge in a creative way.

• Exposure to the significant world

Students in higher education are only a few steps behind the labour force, i.e. the nature of reality. Actual or field visits to familiarise themselves with the processes, interviews with various stakeholder groups, case analysis, small surveys, and so on will enable them to interact closely with the working world.

• Case Study

Though students cannot be exposed to every realistic situation, teachers could use case histories to bring such examples into the classroom. Case studies, as well as thought-provoking questions and exercises, will be shared with them in the classroom or online.

v. **Some novel trends in the assessment and evaluation of BL in the post-covid situation**

In India's post-Covid situation, UGC recommends trying to implement BL as a substitute mode of teaching-learning and thus in the world of assessment and evaluation. The teacher implementing BL mode is expected to consider summative evaluation as another development of formative evaluation. The following sections shed light on some novel evaluation and assessment strategies.

Summative Evaluation Techniques

• **Open book examination:** That is the perfect way to depart from the standard examination approach. This will enable stronger insight and application of knowledge inside the interactive learning system, with a greater potential for positive impact.

• **Group examinations, even for traditional theory papers:** This approach is sometimes used for projects and laboratory assessments. Except in theory-based examinations, it is not generally followed. At first when introduced for theory papers, group examinations can improve the average performance of a category in which students are allowed to discuss their knowledge.

• **Spoken examinations:** With the help of the new generation of technologies, this approach could be implemented. This technique can help students with varying abilities by making examinations faster and easier.

• **On-demand exams:** In most situations, students are required to write in exams. However, these new methods are technology-based, as well as a new combination of teaching-learning and examinations, and it would be a good approach to supply.

• **ePortfolio:** An ePortfolio is not only a compilation of some of the best assignments or activities completed by a learner all through programme, but also his/her reflections on the assigned tasks, his experience and challenges encountered while carrying out these assigned tasks, overall approach, attitude, and ideology towards life as a learner, and also all through his/her academic resume.

• **Innovative Learning methods and Relevant Digital Tools:** Innovative Pedagogies and appropriate ICT Tools facilitate learners to produce creations as a person or group learning activities. These product lines are learning experiences at first, but learners must always provide corrective feedback on their outputs. Once feedback is obtained, learners must be given the opportunity to improve their products before being regarded for formative evaluation.

Classroom/Online Quizzes: Paper-pencil tests and the excessive question-answers discourage formative assessments. However, some Icts for quiz questions and game modes may be used for formative assessments in the future to enhance the learning environment.

• **Use of AI tools for assessments**: In during the post-Covid period, many exams were forced to be administered online. These have been supported by various tools that emerged recently and were proctored using computer science tools. However, AI as a technology is used for a variety of other assessments such as attention levels, learning speed, learning level, and so on.

v. **The BL suggestive measure in a post-covid situation**

BL would be a purposeful combination of online and on-campus learning during the post-pandemic period. UGC inspires higher education teachers in India to develop such BL for at least some of the courses taught in HEIs. The following are some BL-suggestive measures:

The term "online mode of learning" refers to a variety of suggestive measures, including:

1. Obtaining resources, primarily through Open Education

2. Use the teacher-recommended links, manpower, and online databases.

3. The learner studying MOOCs in accordance with the teacher's recommendations.

4. Participating in online virtual meetings with the teacher.

5. Using any ICT tool or platform to carry out individual or group activities.

6. Participating in workshops/webinars as recommended by the teacher.

7. Completing curriculum-related assignments and uploading to LMS / submitting to
teacher

8. Attempting tests/quizzes on other ICT platforms.

9. Participating in virtual learning environments, simulations, museums, and so on.

10. Participation in webinars, e-conferences, and web - based short-term training
programmes.
11. Participating in online internships/projects, etc.
12.Face-to-Face training, fitness training, traineeships, internships, and so on is a
procedure of group classrooms with peer group, as well as trying to apply information
obtained from eResources.
13. Participating in just about any activity conducted course - related curriculum whereby
the student does not need to physically visit the classroom but have to use digital
technology and internet connectivity.

Aside from the measures mentioned above, the IPSIT Model for higher education institutes in India is an efficacious BL measure. Every teacher who wishes to offer his or her course in BL Mode must adhere to all stages of the IPSIT Model.

IPSIT can be broken down as follows:
• Identify Resources and Learner-Centered Activities
• Providing focus on resources and activities on LMS
• Scaffolding and support for learners
• Identifying learning gaps and

• Testing

Conclusion

During the post-pandemic situation in the country, the BL method is used right across the country to help the learners develop 21st-century abilities in addition to effective subject learning and skill development. BL can't be used as a substitute for classroom time. Every institute should strive to be a model institute in order to demonstrate the successful execution of BL in our country's higher education.

Reference

Aji, W., Ardin, H., & Arifin, M. (2020). Blended Learning During Pandemic Corona Virus: Teachers' and Students' Perceptions. *IDEAS: Journal On English Language Teaching And Learning, Linguistics And Literature*, 8(2), 632-646. doi: 10.24256/ideas.v8i2.1696

Beaver, J. K., Hallar, B., & Westmaas, L. (2014, September). Blended learning: Defining models and examining conditions to support implementation. PERC Research Brief. Retrieved from http://8rri53pm0cs22jk3vvqna1ub-wpengine.netdna-ssl.com/

Huang, R., Ma, D., & Zhang, H. (2008). Towards a design theory of blended learning curriculum. In *International Conference on Hybrid Learning and Education* (pp. 66-78). Springer.

Martín-García, A. (2020). *Blended Learning.* Cham: Springer.

Pandit, A. (2020). Blended learning Teaching Techniques in Higher Education in India. *SKIPS Anveshan, 1*(2). doi: 10.53031/skips.1.2.2020.03

Partridge, H., Ponting, D., & MaCay, M. (2011). Good practice report: Blended learning. Retrieved 30 April 2022, from http://eprints.qut.edu.au/47566/1/47566.pdf

Roy, P., & Srivastava, A. (2022). Higher Education 4.0: Digital Revolution for Blended Learning in India. *University News, A Weekly Journal Of Higher Education, Association Of Indian Universities, 60*(4), 24-30.

Stecyk, A. (2018). Teaching quality in blended learning mode. *European Journal Of Service Management, 25,* 297-302. doi: 10.18276/ejsm.2018.25-36

CHAPTER THREE

Usage of Mobile Learning in the Classroom: Benefits and Challenges

Dr. Puja Sarkar*, Mampi Howlader**

* Assistant Professor, Department of Education, The University of Burdwan Gobapbag, Purba Bardhaman-713101, West Bengal, India

** Research Scholar, Department of Education, The University of Burdwan,West Bengal, India

Abstract

The advancement of wireless technology in Education, as well as the creation of mobile apps, is astounding. Because new kinds of devices and apps are transforming Education, it is critical to guarantee that mobile learning is properly used and implemented. Mobile technologies have advanced fast in recent years as a result of advancements in wireless communications, the growth of mobile device capability, and the introduction of open-source mobile platforms. Mobile devices may now be used for more than just communication; they can also be utilised for educational and commercial reasons. Mobile learning has become an important tool to assist and supplement online teaching and learning throughout the pandemic and post pandemic era. For many educational institutions, mobile learning is becoming a crucial concern. Whatever educators and educational institutions do, the introduction of new kinds of technology disrupts Education. As a result, guaranteeing optimal use and implementation of mobile learning requires a comprehensive pedagogical and technical examination. The main directions of mobile learning in teaching and learning are discussed in this chapter. Mobile learning is inadequately disseminated in domestic institutions, despite mobile phones' widespread availability and accessibility among students. The main benefits and some drawbacks of using mobile learning in school are also discussed.

Keywords: Mobile learning; Mobile apps; Education; Technology in Education; Post pandemic period.

Introduction

Mobile technology, such as smartphones, tablets, and laptops, as well as online apps and resources, have become an indispensable part of the lives of most teachers and students throughout the globe in recent decades. People's interaction, information seeking, and work habits have all changed as a result of these technologies. The educators and researchers were given the task of determining how mobile technology may be deployed to improve teaching and learning. The following are some of the potential advantages of mobile technology for learning: promoting learning across settings, contextual learning, and personalization in personal and collaborative situations. Because of these advantages, mobile technology seems to be an exquisite tool for studying mathematics (Cochrane, 2010).

Mobile devices appeal to schools because of their inexpensive cost and a wide variety of features. Devices are often acquired in the hopes of increasing student engagement, which will lead to better learning results. This is based on the premise that students are more likely to acquire positive attitudes when they are fully engaged with assignments. Learning is more likely to occur when people have a positive mindset. Expectations that utilizing such technology will increase student engagement and, as a consequence, result in improved learning outcomes are reflected widely in literature (Beavis, Muspratt, & Thompson, 2015; Chang, Evans, Kim, Norton, & Samur, 2015).

Researchers have created online and mobile apps to aid instruction in Algebra, Geometry, Mathematical Analysis, Statistics, and other fields of mathematics in recent years. Users may investigate functions using mobile math apps, which have graphical capabilities and a variety of calculators. Applications for handling measuring duties as well as instructional apps for improving numerical and mathematical abilities are available. Over the past decade, technologies that facilitate mathematics on the web have also grown in popularity. Mathematical online and mobile teaching technologies may help students solve problems, improve their understanding of mathematical topics, give dynamically represented ideas, and increase general metacognitive skills (Pierce, Stacey, & Barkatsas, 2007). On the one hand, regular use of mobile technology in mathematics would assist students in improving their abilities, while on the other side, it would drive the development of mobile learning apps. Another emerging area of research, according to Heighfield and Goodwin (Highfield & Goodwin, 2013), is the study of the usefulness of mobile applications. So far, the majority of App research has been done by big media organizations, with an emphasis on marketing and device trials. *"Apps for hand-held devices, such as iPads and cell phones, are in tremendous supply,"* according to Larkin (Larkin, 2013). Many of them are math-related. According to a recent search, there are over 4000 applications for math instruction."

This chapter discusses the topic of how mobile technology may be utilized in teaching. It is the student who is at the centre of mobile learning, not the technology. The student is mobile and at the centre of the learning process, and technology enables them to study in any environment. Therefore, the goal of this chapter is to provide various some key aspects of mobile learning. We have also focused on some advantages and disadvantages of mobile learning in brief.

Literature Review

This new method of learning, Mobile learning, has been made possible by recent advancements in mobile and wireless technology (Taleb & Sohrabi, 2012). Educational apps for mobile devices captivate students' attention and inspire them to solve challenges while boosting their memory, reading, and writing abilities. According to mobile learning evaluations (Goh & Kinshuk, 2006), mobile learning may greatly supplement e-learning by providing a second channel of access for users of mobile devices such as headphones, PDAs, MP3, and MP4 players, laptops, and tablets. According to Amelito G. E. (Enriquez, 2010), student surveys demonstrate that students' perceptions of the benefits of utilizing a tablet on their learning experience are overwhelmingly favorable. In recent years, mobile learning has shown to be beneficial in a variety of scenarios and with a variety of target groups. Conway-Smith (Conway-Smith, 2010) reported on a research in South Africa that found a 3.36 percent gain in Math scores over the course of 18 weeks utilising mobile learning. Cook et al. (Crook, Bradley, Lance, Smith, & Haynes, 2007) reported on a mobile learning research in which 73 percent of students said it was critical to learn at any time and from any location. Chu and Liu (Chu & Liu, 2007) performed assessments and found that students believed using mobile devices to study English was beneficial. According to Roberts and Vanska (Roberts & Vänskä, 2011), employing mobile devices improves the motivation and memory of subject content. The outcomes of students' final examinations have also shown some progress. This programme, which aimed at at-risk ninth-grade pupils, helped them concentrate on improving their arithmetic abilities using smartphones. Sobral (Sobral, 2020) conducted a bibliometric review of the widespread use of mobile devices in higher education institutions as an opportunity and a necessity. Alrasheedi, Capretz, and Raza (Alrasheedi, Capretz, & Raza, 2015) did a thorough evaluation of the literature on the elements that affect mobile learning in higher Education. The findings reveal the variables that are required for mobile learning to be accepted successfully. The pandemic, according to Saikat et al. (Saikat, Dhillon, Ahmad, & Jamaluddin, 2021), transformed higher education institutions' (HEIs) perspective of mobile learning as a critical instrument for education delivery. Furthermore, empirical research has shown good satisfaction and behaviour in response to mobile learning in the aftermath of the pandemic (Alturki & Aldraiweesh, 2022).

Characterization of Mobile Learning

A greater understanding of theory-based research is necessary to better comprehend the underlying motivations that cause academics to embrace mobile learning elements and characteristics. So that mobile learning is effective and the implementation is efficient, it is essential that the parts of mobile learning be arranged appropriately and that the interactions between the different aspects are merged efficiently and optimally. Furthermore, the features of mobile learning should be arranged, and how they are applied to mobile learning activities and the application techniques and length of the application time should be prepared ahead of time.

Basic elements of mobile learning are learner, teacher, environment, content and assessment. Figure 1 illustrates the basic elements of an effective mobile learning approach:

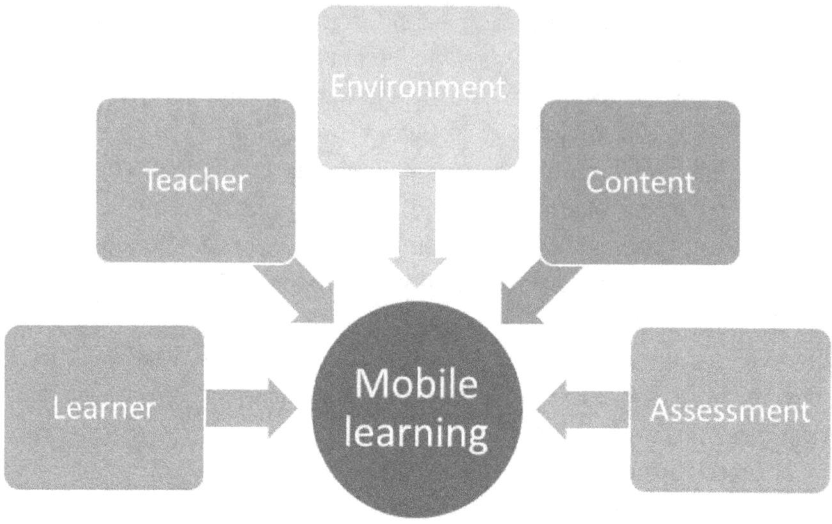

Figure 1: Basic elements of Mobile Learning

Different characterization of mobile learning exists. The ubiquitous, portable size of mobile technologies, blended, private, interactive, collaborative, and instant information are the basic characteristics of mobile learning. According to (Seppälä & Alamäki, 2003), a key feature of mobile learning is that it allows students to be in the appropriate location at the right time, allowing them to feel the real delight of learning. Figure 2 depicts the basic characteristics of a successful mobile learning strategy.

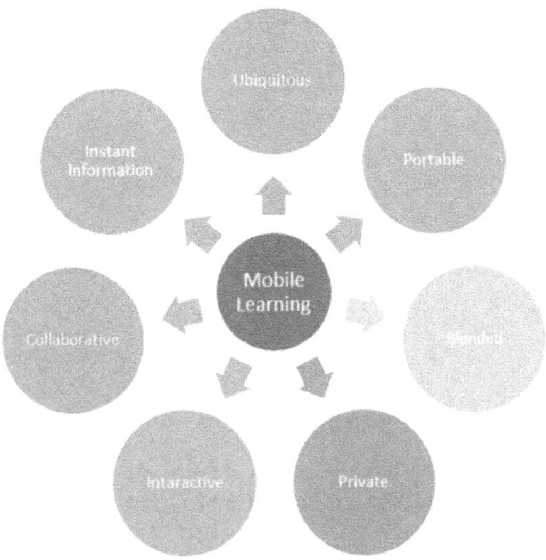

Figure 2: Characterization of Mobile Learning

Advantages of Mobile Learning

All individuals, especially those who live in distant places, may benefit from learning how to utilise mobile devices. To distribute digital information in many countries, mobile devices are the only inexpensive option. One of the most significant changes has occurred with the rise of the so-called "digital natives". Some of the advantages of mobile learning are:

i. Time Efficient

Lack of time is cited as the most significant barrier to workplace learning in LinkedIn's 2018 Workplace Learning Report. By allowing the employee to access information at any time, mobile access immediately tackles this difficulty. Commuting times and leisure between meetings may be utilised productively to learn and grow rather than squandered.

i. Cost-Effective

Traditional classroom-based learning is more expensive than mobile learning. Simply by eliminating the classroom's physical equipment and supplies, as well as the building's real estate costs. When learners utilise their own devices, employers are not obligated to supply them and, as users may complete mobile learning from anywhere, the price and environmental effect of flying to live training sessions is also reduced.

iii. Working remotely

Since mobile learning can be done remotely, it's convenient for students to participate from almost anywhere. In order to accommodate students' other responsibilities, universities provide mobile learning programmes that allow students to engage in distant learning.

iv. User-friendly Learning Environment

Students may easily follow the educational route provided through mobile learning. The use of alerts, updates, and micro-lessons makes it simple to keep tabs on student development. If students are looking for a fun learning experience, SHIFT eLearning recommends this technique above conventional ones.

Challenges of Mobile Learning

Mobile technology, like any other instructional tool, has its drawbacks. According to (Mishra, 2013), there is a slew of obstacles to overcome when introducing and implementing mobile technologies into the classroom.

i. Data Privacy and Security

Learners are often encouraged to use their mobile devices to obtain training while utilising mobile learning. Online training programmes have a tendency to reveal sensitive information about the firm and its employees to the public. As a result, before beginning a mobile training course, a business must first solve the difficulties associated with mobile traffic. Checking for and addressing server vulnerabilities is one approach to achieve this. It may also make it mandatory for all students to install a certain antivirus before accessing the training programme.

ii. Compatibility of Apps

Content compatibility is another issue that learners are likely to face while using mobile learning. The majority of the time, content created for eLearning does not work on mobile devices. In this instance, it will need to renovate or reconstruct them so that mobile learners may access them—this will take time and effort. Aside from that, mobile devices exist in a variety of sizes, requiring content to be prepared in a variety of formats.

iii. Dealing with connectivity and battery life

Although education technology advances at a quick rate, many educational institutions' Internet infrastructures are often overloaded when used by a large number of devices at the same time. As a result, the school administration must guarantee that the school's capacity is up to date.

iv. Avoiding the risk of distraction

Leaving aside the physical aspects, educators must ensure that mobile devices in the classroom are only utilised for educational reasons. Texting with pals, playing games, watching humorous videos, browsing social media channels, and even answering phone calls are all simple tasks for kids. After all, smartphones and tablets are still communication instruments.

Conclusion

Because of the worldwide availability of mobile technology, educators have had the potential for the first time in history to allow anyone from all over the globe to access educational materials, enabling Education for all. Many projects that make educational materials accessible as open educational resources help to enable this. Access to learning is becoming more accessible for anybody who wants to study, thanks to the growing availability of free educational materials via mobile technologies.

More studies should be done in the future to see how mobile learning might revolutionize Education. More rigorous study on the use of mobile technology in learning, according to (Koszalka & Ntloedibe-Kuswani, 2010), is needed to improve the use of mobile learning in Education. In order to improve the application of mobile learning in the twenty-first century, more thorough quantitative and qualitative research studies on mobile learning are required. In the post pandemic era, Education must be modernized to offer instruction utilising mobile technology and to satisfy the demands of 21st-century learners. There is also fear that students' use of mobile devices may lead to more off-task and dangerous conduct. School leaders and legislators will need to design regulations that address safe virtual experiences while still allowing broad access to computing resources. As a result, there will be research possibilities to look at the influence of educational policy on the uptake and integration of mobile learning.

References

Alrasheedi, M., Capretz, L. F., & Raza, A. (2015). A systematic review of the critical factors for success of mobile learning in higher education (university students' perspective). *Journal of Educational Computing Research*, 52(2). https://doi.org/10.1177/0735633115571928

Alturki, U., & Aldraiweesh, A. (2022). Students' Perceptions of the Actual Use of Mobile Learning during COVID-19 Pandemic in Higher Education. *Sustainability (Switzerland)*, *14*(3). https://doi.org/10.3390/su14031125

Beavis, C., Muspratt, S., & Thompson, R. (2015). 'Computer games can get your brain working': student experience and perceptions of digital games in the classroom. *Learning, Media and Technology*, *40*(1). https://doi.org/10.1080/17439884.2014.904339

Chang, M., Evans, M. A., Kim, S., Norton, A., & Samur, Y. (2015). Differential effects of learning games on mathematics proficiency. *Educational Media International*, *52*(1). https://doi.org/10.1080/09523987.2015.1005427

Chu, Y. L., & Liu, T. Y. (2007). Handheld computer supported context-aware learning with 2D barcodes. *Proceedings - The 7th IEEE International Conference on Advanced Learning Technologies, ICALT 2007.* https://doi.org/10.1109/ICALT.2007.154

Cochrane, T. D. (2010). Exploring mobile learning success factors. *ALT-J: Research in Learning Technology*, *18*(2). https://doi.org/10.1080/09687769.2010.494718

Conway-Smith, E. (2010, July 22). Teaching with cell phones. Global Post. *GlobalPost*. Retrieved from https://theworld.org/dispatch/education/100720/south-africa-teaching-cell-phones?page=0,0

Crook, J., Bradley, C., Lance, J., Smith, C., & Haynes, R. (2007). *Generating learning contexts with mobile devices. Mobile learning: Towards a research agenda.* Retrieved from http://www.wlecentre.ac.uk/cms/files/occasionalpapers/mobilelearning

Goh, T. T., & Kinshuk. (2006). Structural equation modelling approach in multiplatform e-learning system evaluation. *ACIS 2006 Proceedings - 17th Australasian Conference on Information Systems.*

Highfield, K., & Goodwin, K. (2013). Apps for mathematics learning: a review of "educational" apps from the iTunes app store. *The 36th Annual Conference of Mathematics Education Research Group of Australasia*, (2009).

Koszalka, T. A., & Ntloedibe-Kuswani, G. S. (2010). Literature on the safe and disruptive learning potential of mobile technologies. *Distance Education, 31*(2). https://doi.org/10.1080/01587919.2010.498082

Larkin, K. (2013). Mathematics Education: Is There an App For That? *Mathematics Education: Yesterday, Today and Tomorrow (Proceedings of the 36th Annual Conference of the Mathematics Education Research Group of Australia).*

Mishra, S. K. (2013). Quality education for children, youth, and adults through mobile learning. In *Pedagogical Applications and Social Effects of Mobile Technology Integration.* https://doi.org/10.4018/978-1-4666-2985-1.ch013

Pierce, R., Stacey, K., & Barkatsas, A. (2007). A scale for monitoring students' attitudes to learning mathematics with technology. *Computers and Education, 48*(2). https://doi.org/10.1016/j.compedu.2005.01.006

Roberts, N., & Vänskä, R. (2011). Challenging assumptions: Mobile learning for mathematics project in South Africa. *Distance Education, 32*(2). https://doi.org/10.1080/01587919.2011.584850

Saikat, S., Dhillon, J. S., Ahmad, W. F. W., & Jamaluddin, R. A. (2021). A systematic review of the benefits and challenges of mobile learning during the covid-19 pandemic. *Education Sciences*, Vol. 11. https://doi.org/10.3390/educsci11090459

Seppälä, P., & Alamäki, H. (2003). Mobile learning in teacher training. *Journal of Computer Assisted Learning, 19*(3). https://doi.org/10.1046/j.0266-4909.2003.00034.x

Sobral, S. R. (2020). Mobile learning in higher education: A bibliometric review. *International Journal of Interactive Mobile Technologies, 14*(11). https://doi.org/10.3991/ijim.v14i11.13973

Taleb, Z., & Sohrabi, A. (2012). Learning on the Move: The use of Mobile Technology to Support Learning for University Students. *Procedia - Social and Behavioral Sciences*, 69. https://doi.org/10.1016/j.sbspro.2012.12.038

CHAPTER FOUR

Post Covid-19 School Education and Opportunities

Dr. Shobha Kalebag, Shuchismita Deb***
** Mahavir Mahavidyalaya, Kolhapur, Maharashtra.*
***, Research Scholar, Department of Education, Shivaji University Kolhapur,*
Maharashtra

Abstract

Covid-19 creates somewhat blunders and somewhere opportunities. At the first time, the whole world suffering a lot in food, fund and barriers of free associations. Covid-19 hampers human life in every sector, but it also has some positive impact on our life. During Covid-19 home isolation makes family integrity. Many of us lost their real moments with loved ones, but it's helped to make a genuine relationship to our dear and near ones. Innovations to stay connected and help each other. A new wave of tools and software that can make this shift to Virtuality. Schools are closed all over the world, but online learning platform most of areas create a new era of education. Only the acute remote areas, there the internet facility were inconvenient, education was seriously problematic. Online classrooms take over institutions can then save infrastructural and overhead expenditure. Covid-19 makes a healthy habit about health and hygiene. Every coin has two faces, bad and good. We are race of survivors, and we are going to win his too.

Key Words: Pandemic, Online class, Covid-19

Introduction:

The school, for many children, is the agent for forming their social connections as well as where early social development occurs. Many families have been impacted negatively by the loss of wages, leading to food insecurity and housing insecurity; some of loss this is a consequence of the need for parents to be at home with young children who cannot attend in-person school. Many families have been impacted negatively by the loss of wages, leading to food insecurity and housing insecurity; some of loss this is a consequence of the need for parents to be at home with young children who cannot attend in-person school. Due to pandemic Graduations, proms, athletic events, college visits, and many other social and educational events have been altered or lost and cannot be recaptured. This crisis has exposed the many inadequacies and inequities in our education systems – from access to the broadband and computers needed for online education, and the supportive environments needed to focus on learning, up to the misalignment between resources and needs. Hanushek and Woessman have used historical growth regressions to estimate the long-run economic impact of this loss of the equivalent to one-third of a year of schooling for the current student cohort. Because learning loss will lead to skill loss, and the skills people have related to their productivity, gross domestic product (GDP) could be 1.5% lower on average for the remainder of the century. School closures in response to the pandemic have shed light on various social and economic issues, including student debt, digital learning, food-insecurity, and homelessness, as-well as access to childcare, health care, housing, internet, and disability services. The impact was more severe for disadvantaged children and their families, causing interrupted learning, compromised nutrition, childcare problems, and consequent economic cost to families who could not work.

The COVID-19 pandemic has affected educational systems worldwide, leading to the near-total closures of schools, early childhood education and care (ECEC) services, universities and colleges.

Most governments decided to temporarily close educational institutions in an attempt to reduce the spread of COVID-19. Learners are currently affected due to school closures in response to the pandemic. According to UNICEF monitoring, 23 countries are currently implementing nationwide closures and 40 are implementing local closures, impacting about 47 percent of the world's student population. 112 countries' schools are currently open.

Closure of schools and the psychological impact on children and adolescents' health, resulting from staying at home for several weeks with uncertain perspectives for the near future, is a crucial is the COVID-19 crisis highlights that school fulfils not only an educational mission of knowledge acquisition, but it also satisfies the socialisation needs of young people.

Absence and despite of the virtual interactions and learning opportunities provided by the internet and social networks, a barrier is created in the educational relationship between pupils and teachers.

Reflection on education during lockdown:

1) Academic integrity:

File-sharing and exam cheating were identified as particularly problematic. Since learning has been the impact on academic integrity has been observed around the world. A rise in contract cheating, academic predominantly remote since the start of the COVID-19 pandemic in March 2020, cheating has become far easier for students. The lack of student to teacher interaction has also led students to feel less passionate about the integrity of their work. This leaves students to turn in half-completed assignments, get the answers from their friends in class, or turn in nothing at all simply because education has become less important due to COVID-19.

2) Gender disparities:

The COVID-19 pandemic has widened the gender gap in education between females and males. Common gender disparities that impact a female's education during the pandemic are finances enabling higher dropout rates, domestic violence, child marriage, early pregnancy, and exploitation of child labor. There is a correlation between increased unemployment rates with higher female school dropout rates. Out of the total population of students enrolled in education globally, UNESCO estimates that over 89% are currently out of school because of COVID-19 closures. Females found challenging in remote learning from face to face to remote online learning; because females are unable to afford internet regularly. For girls getting education is already a struggle. The crisis of gender disparities in education will exceed beyond the pandemic and seep into their future. Lack of Government initiatives in the issue and inability to disparities in education during the pandemic has limited the female education globally.

3) Racial disparities:

Minimal use of internet of school aged children in rural areas. Pandemic has interrupted education across the country, highlighting existing racial and economic inequities. Students in vulnerable neighbourhoods, primarily Black, Indigenous, and other majority-minority areas, faced disparities in everything from resources (ranging from books to counselors) to student-teacher ratios and extracurricular activities.

Even when school closures are temporary, it carries high social and economic costs. The disruptions they cause affect people across communities, but their impact is more severe for disadvantaged children and their families including interrupted learning, compromised nutrition, childcare problems and consequent economic cost to families who cannot afford internet facilities properly.

Impact on formal education:

students impacted by COVID-19 corresponding to the number of learners enrolled at pre-primary, primary, lower-secondary, and upper-secondary levels of education (ISCED levels 0 to 3), as well as at tertiary education levels (ISCED levels 5 to 8).] On average, teachers in K-primary schools were coping worse with the transition than high school educators and university instructors.

Early Childhood care:

Early Childhood cares also hampered by the effect of Covid19. Early childhood educational programmes are usually designed for children below the age of 3 and may refer to preschools, nursery schools, kindergartens, and some day-care programmes. While many primary and secondary schools have closed around the world due to COVID-19, major impacting early childhood educational programmes.

Primary:

Primary or elementary education typically consists of the first four to seven years of formal education. Kindergarten is the first-time children participate in formal education. One study predicted that COVID-19 school closures would slow the rate of literacy ability gain by 66% in kindergarten children in the absence of mitigating alternative educational strategies. One study showing that, kindergarten children would have gained 31% less literacy ability on average than if school closures had not occurred.

Secondary:

Secondary education is in most countries the phase in the education continuum responsible for the development of the young during their adolescence, the most rapid phase of their physical, mental and emotional growth. Due to pandemic situation of Covid19, students of secondary level suffering a lot and their social and emotional wellbeing also hampered. A recent serve The International Baccalaureate Organization (IBO) cancelled the examinations for its Diploma Programme and Career-related Programme candidates scheduled between 30 April and 22 May 2020, reportedly affecting more than 200,000 students worldwide. The IBO stated that it would award candidates their diplomas or certificates based on "their coursework" and "the established assessment expertise, rigor, and quality control already built into the programme. College Board has begun offering both in person and online testing for Advanced Placement exams in the 2020-2021 school yearly citing that 80% of students have experienced some negative impact to their mental health due to the pandemic. Schools and people have lost confidence with the education company and are considering other alternatives for secondary education, and educational reforms are being suggested where students will deviate away from taking significant examinations in the future.

Scope of improvement:

Examine the readiness and choose the most relevant tools: According to UNESCO, use reliable technological solution as local power suppliers, internet connectivity, and digital skills of teachers and students. Through integrated digital learning platforms, video lessons, MOOCs, to broadcasting through radios and TVs.

Ensure inclusion of the distance learning programmes: Students including those with disabilities or from low-income backgrounds have access to distance learning programmes, if only a limited number of them have access to digital devices. Consider them temporarily decentralising such devices from computer labs to families and support them with internet connectivity.

Protect data privacy and data security Assess data security when uploading data or educational resources to web spaces, as well as when sharing them with other organisations or individuals. Ensure that the use of applications and platforms does not violate students' data privacy.

Solutions to address psychosocial challenges before teaching: Make a healthy communication with school, parents, teachers and student. Create communities to ensure regular human interactions, enable social caring measures, and address possible psychosocial challenges that students may face when they are isolated.

Prepare a study plan: Organise discussions with stakeholders to examine the possible duration of school closures and decide whether the distance learning programme should focus on teaching new knowledge or enhance students' knowledge of prior lessons. Plan the schedule depending on the situation of the affected zones, level of studies, needs of student's needs, and availability of parents. Choose the appropriate learning methodologies based on the status of school closures and home-based quarantines. Avoid learning methodologies that require face-to-face communication.

Provide support to teachers and parents on the use of digital tools: Organise training-oriented sessions for teachers and parents, and provide them help to make solutions.

Blend appropriate approaches and limit the number of applications and platforms: Blend tools or media that are available for most students, both for synchronous communication and lessons, and for asynchronous learning. Avoid overloading students and parents by asking them to download and test too many applications or platforms.

Develop distance learning rules and monitor students' learning process: Define the rules with parents and students on distance learning. Design formative questions, tests, or exercises to monitor closely students' learning process. Try to use tools to support submission of students' feedback and avoid overloading parents by requesting them to scan and send students' feedback

Define the duration of distance learning units based on students' self-regulation skills: According to the level of the students' self-regulation and metacognitive abilities especially for live streaming classes. Preferably, the unit for primary school students should not be more than 20 minutes and no longer than 40 minutes for secondary school students.

Build good communication with teacher, student and parents: Make an effective communication with teacher, student and parents and school managers to address sense of loneliness or helplessness, facilitate sharing of experience and discussion on coping strategies when facing learning difficulties.

Online learning platforms

Coursera: With schools closed, demand for online education platforms has increased. Coursera, which can be taught online, also grew significantly during the pandemic.

Coursera saw 59% revenue growth year over year, largely due to a pandemic-induced boom in digital learning.

Total registered users in 2020 grew 65% over 2019:

During the pandemic, Coursera also has partnered with more than 330 government agencies across 70 countries and 30 US states and cities as part of courera.

Others:

Most children have lost substantial instructional time and may not be ready for curricula that were age- and grade- appropriate prior to the pandemic. They will require remedial instruction to get back on track. The pandemic also revealed a stark digital divide that schools can play a role in addressing by ensuring children have digital skills and access.

Areas of action:

The Partners will (i) support the design and implementation of large-scale remedial learning at different levels of education, (ii) launch an open-access, adaptable learning assessment tool that measures learning losses and identifies learners' needs, and (iii) support the design and implementation of digital transformation plans that include components on both infrastructure and ways to use digital technology to accelerate the development of foundational literacy and numeracy skills. Incorporating digital technologies to teach foundational skills could complement teachers' efforts in the classroom and better prepare children for future digital instructions.

Scope for Betterment:

According to UNESCO, UNICEF and World Bank suggest that, all schools provide remedial education.

All schools incorporate social-emotional learning into their teaching.

Proportion of schools offering instruction to develop children's social-emotional skills by level of education.

All schools incorporate digital technology to improve foundational literacy and numeracy skills.

The Partners will collaborate and act at the country level to support governments in accelerating actions to advance the three priorities.

The NGO's and Government social welfare officers' conduct survey to collect data at local, regional and national level, to collect timely data and analytics that provide access to information on school re-openings, learning losses, drop-outs, and transition from school to work, and will make data available to support decision-making and peer-learning. The Partners will join forces in sharing the breadth of international experience and scaling innovations through structured policy dialogue, knowledge sharing, and peer learning actions.

Conclusion:

Covid-19 and lockdown teach the whole world something more than other regular year. In this year we the people faced a lot of problems and life hanging between life and death. In every movement we are scared about the rapid growth of infection and mortality rates. Life is in dangerous situation, education also hampered very much during lockdown. But we all knows that, necessity is the mother of invention, during pandemic education facing problem everywhere, but not stopped, just because the blessings of technology. Technology gives us the online platform of learning. It gives us MOOC, Coursera, Google Classroom, kahoot, Swayam, NIOS and so on; which could help to continue our learning. India is a developing country, where economic conditions of parents are majority poor; so that they can't afford different types of economic gadgets. Only mobile, which are not available in every family especially in rural areas. But within s0o many difficulties education run thoroughly.

Covid-19 teaches us that every problem should have definitely some solutions. During Covid-19 technological assistants was continued to our education virtually in most of the area, which indicates that technology just like blessing of us. If we want to overcome this type of situation, and we have to improve our education system like modern technology oriented, and definitely encourage about blended learning. In every Government school should have technological empowerment. School should encourage E-Learning facilities from urban areas school to acute remote areas too. Implement new released technology in every school. There are many challenges of digital devices, like attendance due to poor network especially in rural areas where internet facilities are inconvenient. Covid-19 enhances lack of social interaction and stigma. Improper internal and external evaluation due to changes in the mode of evaluation. There are so many situations arising and people are faced different types of situations during this pandemic. But a problem makes the man stronger than regular life, and creates potential guts to rearrange the situation, makes the life for betterment.

BIBLIOGRAPHY

Adair Hauck, B. Willingam; McLain, L and Earnest Youngs, B. (1999), "Evaluating the integration of technology and second language learning, CALICO Journal, Vol.17, No.2, Pp.269 – 306

Alla L. Nazarenko (2015), "Blended Learning Vs. Traditional Learning: What Works (A Case Study Research), Procedia – Social and Behavioural

Sciences, Vol.200, Pp.77 – 82, 2015

Anuar MohdYusof; Esther Gnanamalar, S.; Esther Gnanamalar and Norzalita Aziz (2011) investigated into "Teacher's Perceptions on the Blended Learning Environment for Special Needs Learners in Malaysia: A Case Study", Article published by Research Gate (Online)

Arw aAhame dAb do Qasem and G.Viswanathappa (2016) studied "Teacher Perceptions towards ICT Integration: Professional Development through Blended Learning" Journal of Information Technology Education: Research, Vol.15, Pp.561 – 575, 2016

Banados, E. (2006), "A blended learning pedagogical model for teaching and learning EFL successfully through an online interactive multimedia environment, CALICO Journal, Vol.23, No.3, Pp.533 – 550.

Beckem, J.M. and Watkins, M. (2012) in his study "Bringing life to learning - Immersive experiential learning simulations for Online and blended courses", Journal of Asynchronous Learning Networks, Vol.16, No.5, Pp.61 – 70

Beetham, H. And Sharpe, R. (2007), "An introduction to rethinking pedagogy for a digital age", in Beetham, H and Sharpe, R (eds.) Rethinking Pedagogy for a Digital Age, Abingdon, Oxon: Routledge, Pp. 1 – 10.

Benson, V.; Anderson, D. and Ooms, A (2011) probed into 'Educator's Perceptions, Attitudes and Practices: Blended Learning in business and Management Education', Research in Learning Technology, Vol.19, No.2, Pp.143 – 154

Benerjee, G. (2011) made on Blended Environments - Learning effectiveness and students satisfaction at a small college in transition, Journal of Asynchronous Learning Networks, Vol.15, No.1, Pp. 8-19.

Basilaia, G., Kvavadze, D. (2020). Transition to online education in schools during a SARS-CoV-2 coronavirus (COVID-19) pandemic in Georgia. *Pedagogical Research*, 5(4), 10.

Dhawan, S. (2020). Online learning: A panacea in the time of COVID-19 crises. *Journal of Educational Technology*, 49(1), 5–22.

Doucet, A., Netolicky, D., Timmers, K., Tuscano, F. J. (2020). *Thinking about pedagogy in an unfolding pandemic* (An Independent Report on Approaches to Distance Learning during COVID-19 School Closure). Work of Education International and UNESCO.

Dr. Kalebag Shobha and Miss Dabhade Rajaram Pratibha(2021) Covid-19 Pandemic and Dynamics of Higher Education regarding Teaching, learning and evaluation.

Miller, L; Hanfer, C and Ng Kwai Fun, C (2012), "Project-based learning in a technologically enhanced learning environment for second language learners: student's perceptions, E-learning and Digital Media, Vol.9, No.2.

Ravichandran, P., Shah, A. K. (2020 July). Shadow pandemic: Domestic violence and child abuse during the COVID-19 lockdown in India. *International Journal of Research in Medical Sciences*, 08(08), 3118.

Subedi, S., Nayaju, S., Subedi, S., Shah, S. K., Shah, J. M. (2020). Impact of e-learning during COVID-19 pandemic among nurshing students and teachers of Nepal. *International Journal of Science and Healthcare Research*, 5(3), 9.

CHAPTER FIVE

Youth And Covid-19: The Effect of Corona In The 'House' and 'Mind ' of Young Generation

Subratee Bhakat

Guest Lecturer, Rampurhat Teacher Training College, Dist. Birbhum, WB, 731224

Abstract

Global epidemic is a condition that affects people across the globe. This study examined the effects of Covid-19 on the young people and its impact on their mind and economic conditions of their family. Accordingly in this study social condition and the mind set of young generation due to the effect of Covid-19 have been fallen into account. This study is an analysis on the review of paper related to the topic and the papers related to the impact of the Covid-19 on people. Secondary sources were used for collection of data. The findings revealed that there is a negative impact of Covid-19 condition on the young generation and it has also affected their physical and mental health. However, the possibility of a new beginning in the aftermath of any crisis is immense.

Keywords: Anxiety, Depression, Stress, Pandemic.

Introduction

People from all walks of life have been affected in various ways since the epidemic due to Covid-19, men and women, young generation, rich and poor, irrespective of caste and creed, have all been affected in different ways. The main areas where Covid-19 has had a serious negative impact on young people are their workplaces, education, rights and mental health.

The catastrophe started in December 2019, from this time onwards, the Nobel coronavirus began to have far-reaching effects. This virus has changed the socio-economic and health scenario of the whole world. In our country the government has announced emergency shutdowns in almost all the states since March 2020. Then a long time passes, social stagnation is created. Covid-19 caused a worldwide economic downturn due to its rapid and unprecedented spread. As a result, jobs and businesses of people are at risk. This epidemic has taken a heavy toll on human life and also the lives of the younger generation. History has shown us how long and severe a crisis like an epidemic can be for a young population. For example, the global youth unemployment rates grew due to financial crisis in 2008 and has yet to return to pre-crisis levels).

The younger generation (age group,18-29) covers a large part of our society. At this age young people are involved in various activities and they have to prove themselves as the greatest force of mankind and social progress. According to India's 2011 Census report, 19% of the total population belongs to the age group of 18-29, young population. Thus, the question remains how this huge segment of Indian population is affected by the global epidemic crisis and what is the nature of impact of the crisis on their mental health.

More over serious impact of Covid-19 has been found in the areas of education, employment, economic condition and human relation. Severe uncertainty have been found in the field of education, workplace and daily lives of the workers. The Global Survey on Youth and COVID-19's highlights four areas of impact of the epidemic on youth: employment, education and training, mental health, and human right. This study is an analysis about the impact of Covid-19 on the four areas and its interrelationship with the young generation.

Review of Literature

Some of the available reports were received by the researcher to indicate the nature of impact of Covid-19 on the people of different countries and different categories

- Rashid, A. A.(2020)- In this article the management system of developed and developing countries in the situation of pandemic. The pandemic has taught us many things. In fact, many of the norms and rules for the cities can manage infectious diseases.

- A Global Report of International Labour Organization, (2020)- stated the effects of the pandemic on the lives of young people with regard to employment, education, mental well-being, rights and social activism, in a very comprehensive manner.
- Tackling Coronavirus, Contributing to a Global Effort (2020)- OCED policy responses to Coronavirus in its report on the Global Health emergency and its economic and social impacts mentioned that nearly all aspects of life of all sections in society have disrupted due to Covid-19. Based on the survey findings from 80 youth organizations of 48 countries, this policy briefly outlines the practical measures. Those can be adopted by the government for inclusive and fair recovery measure.
- Lee, J. et.al (2021)- Conducted a study on the impacts of Covid-19 on the mental health of USA college students. Findings of the study indicates that the students closer to graduating faced increases in anxiety, feeling of loneliness and depression.

Objective

1. To estimate the effects of epidemic on the young generation's mind.
2. To study the impact of epidemic on their life of young generation.
3. To find out the relationship between the impact of Covid-19 and the income and livelihood pattern of young generation.
4. To identify the new challenges faced by the young generation during Covid-19 situation.

Methodology

The article on youth and Covid-19 and its effects on the 'house' and the 'mind' of young generation is a critical analysis of various write up related to the topic based on the secondary sources of information. In this connection the approach of critical appraisal was adopted by the author to highlight the scenario about the impact of Covid-19 on the young generation.

Discussion

Effect of Corona in the 'House' of Young People

The young generation between the ages of 18 and 29 are standing in a place where they have to make sure that their future path is determined by which ways, they will lead their life. Young people who decide to take on all the responsibilities of their family and move on. In both cases, there is a significant loss of life at this crucial juncture. Those who decide to pursue higher education had to wait almost two years. Those who take responsibility for their families for various reasons had to face a different kind of problem. In the midst of the Corona situation and the long stagnation of society, income opportunities continue to decline, and in some cases even employee layoffs have been reported. This condition causes them various problems.

there have been found both direct and indirect effect on the lives of young people. The author in her article would like to name this effect as the Effect of COVID-19 in the 'House and Mind of Young People'. Those who prepared themselves for higher education and wanted to see themselves established and successful just in time are far behind due to effect of the epidemic. If we try to understand the matter in depth, we could observe that the dependence of all those young men and women on their families has increased and that creates some pressure on the family. On the other hand, those who have taken over the responsibility of the family facing serious financial problems. As a result, serious disruption have been found in the normal life of young generation due to the effects of Covid-19. Here the author wants to use the word 'in house' in the metaphorical sense of various problems caused by financial shortage. More over Corona was affected young workers and students in the following ways

1. The closure of schools, universities and training centers effected over 73 percent of the youth who were in Education or training (Youth and Covid-19 survey report).
2. Share of Youth (aged18-29) reported that their studies or training had been interrupted since onset of the pandemic.

3.Since the beginning of the epidemic, young students and staff have seen their education and training centers completely closed without any function of education.

All of the above factors have significant impact on the lives of young students. That has not only affected them, but also brought danger to their families. Various problems such as financial shortage, lack of adequate food and necessities, cost of education or training, inability to procure necessary equipment and soon have created danger for both young generation and their families.

Effects of corona in 'Mind ' of the young

This catastrophe has not been ended with mere external damage. It has caused deep wounds in the minds of the youth. Issues such as employment problems, loss of income, etc. have affected the mental health of the youth in different ways. It is natural that the epidemic and the socio-economic situation are integrated and have impact on the life of people as well as young generation. But to estimate the nature of impact a critical analysis is essential which has been made by the author.

The mental health of young people has suffered the most since the onset of the epidemic. Many of the young workers have lost their jobs. Those who were involved in various types of vocational training had their educational institutions shut down, doubling their anxiety and depression. Mental health in times of crisis is somewhat related to age. Anxiety and depression are more prevalent in young people between the ages of 18 and 29 than in adults. They are prone to depression and anxiety. The reasons that have arisen among the youth during the crisis are: the long-running school closures and work closures, the sudden dangers in their families and the separation of loved ones and the epidemic that surrounds them.

The survey report on the youth and Covid-19, indicates that 38% of young people in the world are uncertain and 16% fearful about their future and career prospects. In such a situation young people compelled to realise that their future has been affected by epidemics, closer of schools and exams related activity. In this condition the ambitions of young men which is largely determined by the external environment have affected seriously. The adverse effects of the epidemic have increased their fears and anxieties. As a result, young people today are emotionally broken and their mental health has deteriorated.

Impacts of COVID-19 on college students

A large part of the youth are college students. It is necessary to estimate the effect of this epidemic on the students of the college. Knowing the impact on their physical and mental health, college students come across various issues and their feelings. A review of data from a survey of over 200 colleges in the US found that factors affecting the mental health of college students include an increase in fear, depression, and loneliness among students.

Mental Health	**Percentage**
Increase anxiety	60.8
Increase depression	54.1
Increased feelings of loneliness	59.8
Concerned about the health of loved ones	20

Fig: Ways in which COVID-19 has affected the mental health of college students

The above report shows that 60.8 % of the respondents reported an increase in anxiety, 54.1 % reported increased depression 59.8 % reported increased feelings of loneliness and about 20% are concerned about the health of the loved ones, school/ education and lack of productivity.

Findings

In light of the above discussion, it is very clear that the effects of the epidemic have had a negative impact on our people and the youth. "Young people are less at risk of severe disease and death from Covid-19 but will be the most affected by the long-term consequences of the pandemic which will save the world they leave and the work in for decades to come".- Said Dr Tedros Adhanom Ghebreyesus, Director General of the World Health Organization(WHO). In other words, its impact on the lives of young people is not temporary, it will also bring changes in the way of life in the future.

During the epidemic, young people are emotionally backward due to the sudden closure of their employment opportunities and various education and training centers. They have faced various forms of discrimination. Young people identified as ethnic, religious or other minority have felt the impact more and more. Infinite conflict is going on between the physical and mental of the youth. Many have not yet recovered from the effects of the crisis, which has affected the health and mental health of young people in many ways.

Infinite conflict is going on between the physical and mental of the youth. Many have not yet recovered from the effects of the crisis, which has affected the health and mental health of young people in many ways.

Conclusion

However, the possibility of a new beginning in the aftermath of any crisis is immense. This period can be called the period of waking up. Sustainable social systems can be built with new opportunities and possibilities. The ability of young people to deal with problems and to think long and hard increases, and in many cases bad habits are replaced by good ones. They can establish themselves in the society in different ways by facing the current situation. These are the opportunities that lie ahead-

Scaling up online/ remote learning skilling and livelihood platforms will help them advancing employment entrepreneurship and civic engagement opportunities.

Entrepreneurship skills and opportunities will provide the necessary support for the establishment of local entrepreneurial education and culture for young people.

Young people play the basic role as change makers. The Covid-19 situation will help and support young people as change maker and co-creator of their own solutions.

References

Rasid, A., A.,(2020), Covid-19:The End of Global Sustainable Cities? *URBANICE*. Malaysia

Retrieve from: https://www.academia.edu/42653168/ COVID-19_THE_END_OF_GLOBAL_SUSTAINABLE_CITIES

YOUTH & COVID-19: Impacts On Jobs, Education, Rights And Mental Well-Being,(2020), *Decent Jobs For Youth*, ILO(11 August,2020).

Retrieved From: https://www.ilo.org/global/topics/youth-employment/publications/WCMS_753026/lang--en/index.htm

Special Issue On COVID-19 And Youth, (2020), Produced by the Programme on youth unit, Division for inclusive social Development, Department of Economics and Social Affaires, United Nation.

Retrieved from: https://www.un.org/development/desa/dspd/wp-content/uploads/sites/22/2020/04/YOUTH-FLASH-Special-issue-on-COVID-19-1.pdf

Youth and Covid-19: Response ,Recovery, Resilience,(2020), OECD.

Retrieved From: https://www.oecd.org/coronavirus/policy-responses/ youth-and-Covid-19-response-recovery-and-resilience-c40e61c6/

Youth Are Leading The Charge To A Brighter Post-COVID World, (2021), WHO

Retrieved From: https://www.who.int/news-room/feature-stories/detail/youth-are-leading-the-charge-to-a-brighter-post-covid-world

Lee,J., Solomon, M., Stead,T., Kwon ,B.,& Ganti, L.,(2021), Impact Of COVID-19 On The Mental Health Of US College Students, *BMC Psycology*.
Retrieved From: https://bmcpsychology.biomedcentral.com/articles/10.1186/s40359-021-00598

Mental health and its impact on academic achievement among the Post Graduate girls' hostel boarders of Cotton University after Covid 19 situation

Jinti Kalita*, Dr. Phunu Das Sarma**

*Ex – student, Cotton University, Assam

** Associate professor, Department of Education, Cotton University, Assam

Abstract : This research study has explored the mental health of the post graduate girl's hostel boarders of Cotton University after the Covid 19 situation using descriptive survey method. The study includes the mental health of these students and it's impact on their academic achievements. It is very necessary to maintain a good mental health of the students to achieve their desired educational outcomes. Hostels are the first place where the students have to stay without their parents for a considerable period for educational purposes. Here they are faced with new situations, new problems, new people, new rules and regulations which can affect their mental health adversely. The COVID-19 disease itself, and its effects of quarantine and nationwide lockdowns have induced acute panic, anxiety, obsessive behaviours, depression, and may also lead to post- traumatic stress disorder (PTSD) in the long run. From the study it has been shown that majority of the students have good mental health and it is impacting their academic life in a positive way. Good mental health can provide support to the students to perform well to achieve their academic goals.

Introduction :

In recent years, mental health of individuals has taken considerable attention worldwide, because of a dramatic upward trend in suicide. It is estimated to account for a large burden of disease than any other class of health conditions.

When the students struggle with mental health problems, they often have attendance problems, difficulty in completing assignments, increased conflicts with adults and peers. Mental health problems have negatively impact our academic productivity and interpersonal relationships.

Students displaying strong mental health are likely to have better academic achievement, compared to the students displaying weak mental health. Individuals showing strong mental health have good social skills with both adults and peers.

Therefore, mental health problems may have an important influence on the academic achievements of the students, which in turn have lifelong consequences for employment, income and other outcomes. Early recognition and interventions are highly valuable in this matter.

University students are one of the most sensitive strata of society, many of whom will become the future's managers and planners, and the mental health of the society is contingent upon their mental health. Challenges of the university years can bring students sources of anxiety, hence endangering their health.

During the last decade, university and college counselling centres reported a shift in the need of students seeking counselling services from different kinds of developmental issues to more severe psychological problems. Hence it is very important to maintain a good mental health for the students and to identify it's related problems.

Need of the study :

The study of mental health and its impact on academic achievement is important for several reasons. An inverse relationship between mental health and academic achievement is well- known phenomenon in the scientific literature.

Research shows that high levels of mental health are associated with increased learning, creativity and productivity, more pro-social behaviour and positive social relationships, and with improved physical health and life expectancy.

At times, we all experience personal difficulties that may cause disruption and confusion in our lives. Study usually involves a significant commitment of time and effort and requires a disciplined routine in order to achieve academic success, which can place significant stress on mental health. In the same way, mental health issues can pose a huge problem for students in terms of academic and social success in school. Peers, family members, faculty and stuff may be personally affected out of concern for these students with mental health problems. So, there is a great need of studying this area of our lives.

Statement of the study :

"Mental health and it's impact on academic achievement among the Post Graduate girl's hostel boarders of Cotton University after covid 19 situation"

Objectives of the study :

a) To know the present mental health condition of the students.

b) To ascertain the impact of mental health on the academic achievements of the students.

Operational definition :

a. **MENTALHEALTH** : Mental health is our emotional, psychological and social well-being. It affects how we think, feel and act.

b. **MENTALHEALTHPROBLEMS** : Mental illness, also called as mental health problems or disorders refers to a wide range of mental health conditions – disorders that affect our mood, thinking and behavior.

c. **ACADEMICACHIEVEMENT** : Academic achievement is the extent to which a student, teacher or institution has attained their short or long-term educational goals. Completion of educational benchmarks such as secondary school diplomas and bachelor's degrees represent academic achievement.

Delimitation of the study :

The study is restricted to only the Post graduate girl's hostel boarders of Cotton University (Guwahati). This study is conducted to know about the mental health of these students of Cotton University and it's impact on their academic achievements.

Description of the area :

Guwahati is the biggest city of Indian state of Assam and also the largest metropolis in Northeastern India. Cotton University, Guwahati is located at Panbazar, Guwahati, Kamrup, Assam. It was established in 2017 by the provision of an act enacted by Assam Legislative Assembly to merge the Cotton College State University and Cotton College. Dr. Kamala Roy Girl's hostel, Swahid Kanaklata Girl's Hostel and Nalinibala Devi Girl's Hostel are the Girl's hostels for the post graduate students of Cotton University all of which are situated near Digholipukhuri, Guwahati, Assam.

Review of related literature

a. Anand S.P (1989) conducted a study on mental health of high school students. The main objective of the study was to find out the mentally healthy and unhealthy students and to find out the relation between parental education and occupational status. It was found that mental health of children was dependent upon education and occupational status of parents. Sound mental health was positively related to academic achievement and both of them were positively related to parental status. The degree of mental health was also related to the type of school, being the highest in the convenient schools, followed by Sainik DAV and DM schools, respectively.

a. Bhugendranath Panda (1989) conducted a study on mental health personal adjustment and Saora Acculturation (a cross-cultural study) in secondary school students, boys and girls. The main objective of the study was to study the independent and interactive effects of acclimation and sex on mental health score of Oriya children.

He found that, Oriya groups posses better social adjustment than other groups, and there does not any difference between all other group combinations in their mental health.

c. Prasanna K.C.B (1989) conducted a study on certain mental health variables associated with high and low achieving adolescents.

- It studied that all mental health variables studied discriminated between high and low achievers in most of the group studies.
- High achievers had higher mean scores than low achievers for all the 16 mental health variables studied. The findings of the study indicate the need

- Avoid threats which caused disequilibrium in children.
- To provide for guidance-oriented teaching.
- To organize extension lectures for parents and community.
- To form parent-teacher association and to encourage pupils to participate in extracurricular activities and institutional guidance.

d. Jangannadhan.K. conducted a study on the effects of certain social psychological factors on the academic achievements of children studying in classes V to VII PhD EDV-SVD-1985. The major findings were-

- The inter correlations between social psychological variables showed that, home environment had a positive and significant correlation with other independent factor. The relationship of home environment with socio economic status and school environment was significant it 0.5 percent.
- Home environment yielded a correlation of 0.042 with academic achievement and was found highly significant.

e. Myron (2008) conducted a study on child and adolescent mental disorders to describe objectively the global gaps in policy, data gathering capacity and resources to develop and implement services to support child mental health. The study showed that current global epidemiological data consistently reports that up to 20% of children and adolescents suffer from a disabling mental illness; that suicide is the third leading cause of death among adolescents; and that up to 50% of all adult mental disorders have their onset in adolescence.

f. Kumar and Singh (2007) studied the role stress among professional students in India. The finding reveals that male students experienced higher levels of role stagnation than female students. However, no significant differences could be observed on any of the role stressors between first year students and their seniors, or between management and engineering students.

g. Agolla and Ongori (2009) carried out a study on "An assessment of academic stress among

undergraduate students: The case of University of Botswana." It was found that academic

workload, inadequate resources, low motivation, poor performance in academic, overcrowded lecture halls and uncertainty of getting job after graduation from the university lead to stress among students.

h. Kadapatti, Manjula & Vijayalaxmi (2012) carried out a study to know the stressors of Academic Stress among pre-university students. The results of this study showed that high aspiration, more study problems, change in medium of instruction, poor study habits & low socio-economic conditions are the responsible factors for to academic stress and become stressors for stress among selected respondents.

In this chapter, the literature related to the study was dealt in depth. The search of related literature helped much to have a proper prospective of the problem chosen for the study. Further it has helped the investigator to formulate methodology and a well- planned procedure for the investigation.

Research Methodology

The research methodology means a kind of guidelines for solving a problem with special components such as tasks, methods, rules and postulates employed by discipline.

Methods used in the study :

The investigator used descriptive survey method in the study. Descriptive survey method was used to collect detailed information of existing phenomena. A self structured questionnaire was applied to fulfil the aim of the study.

Population :

The present study deals with the hostel boarders of Dr. Kamala Roy girls' hostel, Swahid Kanaklata girls' hostel and Nalinibala Devi girls' hostel of Cotton University, Guwahati. The total population of the students of post graduation level of these hostels is 70.

Sample :

The investigator selected 40 PG hostel boarders of the University randomly. Therefore, the technique used to select the sample was random sampling.

Tools used in the study :

The tool used in the study is questionnaire.

Questionnaire : A questionnaire consists of a variety of the printed or typed statements or questions in a definite form.

Data collection :

The investigator had an informal visit at the hostels of Cotton University, Guwahati. The investigator met the hostel boarders personally and interacted with them to make them comfortable. Then the investigator distributed the questionnaires among them and requested them to provide their responses without hesitation.

Analysis and Interpretation

For analysis and interpretation of the data for the present study on the basis of the objectives are given as following –

Analysis of the first objective : **To know the present mental health condition of the students.**

Statement No.	Statements	Responses			Percentage of Responses		
		Agree	Undecided	Disagree	Agree	Undecided	Disagree
1	I lead a peaceful life in the hostel.	33	6	1	82.5%	15%	2.5%
2	There is no hazardous condition present in my hostel.	32	7	1	80%	17.5%	2.5%
5	We have proper environment for studying in the hostel.	35	5	0	87.5%	12.5%	0%
7	I have never found any difficulty in participating in the class activities due to health problems.	24	9	7	60%	22.5%	17.5%
13	I feel good about myself.	32	8	0	80%	20%	0%
14	I am positive about my life.	28	10	2	70%	25%	5%

Table 1 - <u>Mental satisfaction of the students</u>

Interpretation of table no. 1 :

The interpretation of table no. 1 is discussed below –

a. Table no. 1 shows that 82.5% of the total students are leading a Peaceful life in the hostel and 2.5% of the students are not leading a peaceful life in the hostel, whereas 15% of the students are undecided about it. Hence, it has seen that majority of the students are leading a peaceful life in the hostel.

b. 80% of the students agree that there is no hazardous condition present in their hostel, whereas 2.5% of the students disagree with it and 17.5% are undecided about it. It refers that there is a comparatively good environment in the hostel.

c. 87.5% of the students agree that there is proper environment for studying in the hostels, while 12.5% of the students are undecided about it, and nobody was disagree with it. In this case, it is observed that hostels are successful in providing good study environment to the students.

d. 60% of the students agree that they have never found any difficulty in participating in the class activities due to health problems, 22.5% of the students were undecided about it and 17.5% of the students notified that they found difficulty in participating in the class activities due to health problems. Here, it seems that health problems interfere with the eager of these 17.5% of the students to participate in the class activities.

e. From the table it is observed that 80% of the students feel good about themselves and 20% of them are undecided about it. There was nobody who doesn't feel good about himself or herself. So it is observed that there is self satisfaction among the students.

f. 70% of the students are positive about their lives, while 25% of the students are undecided about it and 5% of the students disagree with it. As positivity is an essential aspect for mental health, there is a need to take steps to make these students positive about their lives.

Statement No.	Statements	Agree	Undecided	Disagree	Agree	Undecided	Disagree
8	I have experienced some mental complaints in the past.	8	7	25	20%	17.5%	62.5%
11	I feel low or down very often.	15	10	15	37.5%	25%	37.5%
12	My mental health affects my relationship with people.	10	10	20	25%	25%	50%
19	I feel frustrated when the discussion is interrupted during a class or when the teacher is absent.	10	14	16	25%	35%	40%
20	During examination I feel more frustrated.	20	8	12	50%	20%	30%
24	I become easily annoyed or irritable.	11	5	24	27.5%	12.5%	60%

Table 2 - Mental peace of the students

Interpretation of table no. 2 :

The interpretation of table no. 2 is discussed below-

a. The table no. 2 shows that only 20% of the students have experienced some mental complaints in the past, although 17.5% of the total students are undecided about it. The 62.5% of the students disagree with it and are of the opinion that they have never experienced any kind of mental complaints in the past.

b. 37.5% of the students reported that they feel low or down very often. 25% of the students are undecided about it. Whereas 37.5% of the students also reported that they do not feel low or down very often. In this aspect, the percentage of students who oftenly feel low or down is equal to the percentage of the students who do not feel low or down very often.

c. The table shows that 25% of the students admit that their mental health affect their relationship with people, equally on the other hand 25% of the students are undecided about it. Majority is there in the students with 50% who admits that their mental health don't affect their relationship with people. It refers that majority of the students have control on their emotions and thoughts.

d. 25% of the students feel frustrated when the discussion is interrupted during a class or when the teacher is absent, although 35% of them are undecided about it. 40% of the students doesn't feel frustrated in the same case.

e. 50% of the students feel more frustrated during examinations, 20% of them are undecided about it and 30% of the students admits that they do not feel more frustrated during examinations. It refers that majority of the students feel more frustration during examinations.

f. It is seen that 60% of the students do not become easily annoyed or irritable, whether 12.5% of them are undecided about it. Only 27.5% of the students admit that they become easily annoyed or irritable. It indicates that most of the students are not easily annoyed.

Statement No.	Statement	Responses			Percentage of Responses		
		Agree	Undecided	Disagree	Agree	Undecided	Disagree
3	I have regular contact with my parents.	38	0	2	95%	-	5%
4	My parents visit my hostel regularly.	7	11	22	17.5%	27.5%	55%
9	The persons with whom I am frequently in contact with help me to overcome my fears.	34	5	1	85%	12.5%	2.5%
25	I feel confident in front of my teachers.	22	11	7	55%	27.5%	17.5%
26	I have my own goals for studying this particular course.	35	4	1	87.5%	10%	2.5%
29	Compared with the average students in my class, I am doing well in my academic activities.	16	15	9	40%	37.5%	22.5%

Table 3 - Mental support of the students

Interpretation of the table no 3 :
The interpretation of the table no. 3 are discussed below –

a. It is observed that 95% of the students have regular contact with their parents. Only 5% of the students do not have regular contact with their parents. It refers that there is very good parents'- children relationship among them.
b. 17.5% of the students admits that their parents regularly visit their hostels. Although 27.5% of them are undecided about it, the majority 55% of the students report that their parents do not visit their hostels regularly. It refers that there is a lack of communication between the parents and the children.

c. The table shows that 85% of the students are able to overcome their fears with the help of the persons with whom they are frequently in contact with. Though, 12.5% of the students are undecided about it. Only 2.5% of the students reported it negatively. It indicates that majority of the human relations that the students are possessing are helping them in overcoming their fears.

d. 55% of the students feel confident in front of their teachers. 27.5% of the students are undecided about it. 17.5% of the students admit that they do not feel confident in front of their teachers.

e. 87.5% of the students have their own goals for studying their particular course, whereas 10% of the students are undecided about it. The rest 2.5% of the students admits that they do not have any particular goal for studying their own course. It refers that majority of the students have their own particular goals for studying their particular course, which will help them in achieving their desired academic outcomes.

f. It is observed that 40% of the students believe that they are doing well in their academic activities, compared with the average students of the class. 37.5% of the students are undecided about it and the rest 22.5% of the students admit that they are not doing well in their academic activities compared with the average students of their class.

Statement No.	Statement	Agree	Undecided	Disagree	Agree	Undecided	Disagree
6	I participate in the various activities of the class.	21	9	10	52.5%	22.5%	25%
10	I can handle my problems graciously.	27	10	3	67.5%	25%	7.5%
15	I can concentrate on my studies very effectively.	20	15	5	50%	37.5%	12.5%
22	I help my friends in studying.	38	2	0	95%	5%	0%
23	I can control worrying.	20	13	7	50%	32.5%	17.5%
28	I am able to make my own decisions.	32	6	2	80%	15%	5%

Table no. 4 - Problem solving ability of the students

Interpretation of the table no. 4 :

The interpretation of table no. 4 is discussed below :

a. 52.5% of the students participate in the various activities of the class, although 22.5% of the students are undecided about it. The rest 25% of the students admits that they do not participate in some activities of the class. It refers that students participation in the various activities of the class is not so strong, although majority lies there.

b. It is observed that 67.5% of the students can handle their problems graciously. 25% of the students are undecided about it and 7.5% of the students says that they can not handle their problems graciously. It refers that majority of the students have good skill to handle problems effectively.

c. The table shows that 50% of the students can concentrate on their studies effectively. The rest 37.5% and 12.5% of the students are undecided and can not concentrate on their studies accordingly. Which refers only half of the students concentrates on their studies effectively.

d. 95% of the students admit that they help their friends in studying. Only 5% of the students are undecided about it and there not lies anyone who doesn't help their friends in studying. It refers majority of the students are helpful and makes their abilities useful for others also.

e. 50% of the students admit that they can control worrying. The rest 32.5% of the students are undecided about it and 17.5% of the students can not control worrying about anything. It seems that almost half of the students have good control over their thoughts and emotions.

f. The table shows that 80% of the students are able to make their own decisions. Whereas 15% of the students are undecided about it and the rest 5% of the students can not make their own decisions. It indicates that majority of the students make their own decisions.

<u>Analysis of the second objective</u> : To ascertain the impact of mental health on the academic achievements of the students.

Statement No.	Statement	Agree	Undecided	Disagree	Agree	Undecided	Disagree
16	I am happy with the results of my educational assessment.	26	7	7	65%	17.5%	17.5%
17	I do my assignments regularly.	38	2	0	95%	5%	0%
18	I attentively listen to the lectures of my professors.	35	3	2	87.5%	7.5%	5%
21	I explore more effort in doing my difficult assignments.	33	4	3	82.5%	10%	7.5%
27	I want to reach my academic goal without hampering others.	40	0	0	100%	0%	0%
30	I set deadlines for myself for completing my classwork.	28	11	1	70%	27.5%	2.5%

<u>Table no. 5</u>

Interpretation of the table no. 5 :

The interpretation of the table no. 5 are discussed below :

a. The table shows that 65% of the students are happy with their results of academic assessments. The rest of the students are equally divided i.e. 17.5% and 17.5% who are undecided and not happy with their results. It seems that there is the presence of academic achievement for the majority of the students.

b. 95% of the students have admitted that they do their assignments regularly. Only 5% of the students are undecided about it and there is no one who doesn't do their homework or assignments regularly. It refers that there is punctuality among the students.

c. 87.5% of the students have reported that they attentively listen to the lectures of their professors. 7.5% of the students are undecided about it and 5% of the students do not listen to the lectures of their professors attentively. It refers that the strong mental health of the majority of the students are definitely helping them in moving towards achieving their desired academic goal.

d. It is seen that 82.5% of the students explore more effort in doing their difficult assignments, whereas 10% of the students are undecided about it and 7.5% of the students admit that they do not explore more effort in doing their difficult assignments. Hence, the problem solving ability of the majority of the students is very good and helps them to try it more.

e. The table shows that 100% of the students want to reach their academic goal without hampering others. It reflects the presence of strong mental health and positivity among all the students.

f. 70% of the students admits that they set deadlines for themselves for completing their classwork. Whereas 27.5% of the students are undecided about it and 2.5% admits that they do not set deadlines for completing their classwork. It seems that majority of the students are dedicated to their works.

Findings of the study

After analysis and interpretation of the study, the following points may be mentioned as the findings of the study :

a. Majority of the hostel boarders are leading a peaceful life in their hostels. Most of them agrees that there is no hazardous condition present in their hostels.

b. Hostels are successful in providing good study environment to students. Majority of the boarders opined the environment in a positive way.

c. Though there are few students who finds difficulty in participating in class activities due to health problems, majority of them were found to be physically fit.

d. Majority of the students feel good about themselves and are positive towards their lives, which indicates the presence of strong mental satisfaction among the students.

e. Most of the students have never experienced any kind of mental complaints in the past, though half of them are found to feel low or down very often.

f. The relationship of the majority of the students are not affected by their mental health and majority of them do not become easily annoyed or irritable.

g. Majority of the students do not feel frustrated when the discussion is interrupted during a class or when the teacher is absent, though many of them admits that they feel more frustrated during examinations.

h. There is very good parent-child relationship among the hostel boarders and their parents, though it was found that majority of the parents do not visit them in their hostels regularly.

a. Majority of the students are able to overcome their fears with the help of their close persons and feel confident in front of their teachers.

j. Most of the students have their own goals for studying their particular course and believe that they are doing well in their academic activities.

k. Majority of the students have very good problem solving ability and dealing with their academic life very effectively.

ax. Majority of the students are happy with their results of academic assessments and they are doing their best to achieve more.

Conclusion

Poor mental health can effect students at all stages of their university experience. Whether they are facing loneliness, anxiety or even depression, mental health difficulties can have significant impact on a student's ability to engage with their studies, make friends and make the most of university experiences.

Hence, the present study has focused on understanding the mental health of the post graduation level hostel boarders as they live away from their homes and have to deal with various situations of their own. In this competitive scenario, mental health has become a major indicator of a person to be successful. The role of the students in the development of the societies and the nations, as a whole is very important. Hence, it felt that there is the presence of very strong mental health among the post graduate hostel boarders of cotton university and they are successfully achieving their desired academic goals after the Covid 19 situation also.

Suggestions

Based on the findings of the study, the investigator would like to suggest the following measures for better mental health among the students :

a. Some motivational sessions can be organized to bring more positivity among the students about their lives. Motivational speeches are always helpful in bringing positivity among the people.

b. Parents should visit their children in the hostel frequently, as their warmth can always make the children happy.

c. Hostel authorities should also visit the hostels sometimes so that they can know if there is anything wrong and take the preventive measures for the benefit of the students.

Bibliography

a. Adams., H. E., Psychology of Adjustment, New York: Ronald, 1972
b. Arkoff, Abe, Adjustment and Mental Health, New York:McGraw-Hill, 1968,P.6.
c. Carroll, H. A., Mental Hygiene: The dynamics of adjustment, N. J. : Prentice-Hall, 1967
d. Goswami Dr. Sadhana, Statistics in Education, Shanti Prakashan
e. KaulLokesh, Methodology of Educational Research, Vikash publishing house, pvt. Ltd.
f. Singh SiddhuKulbir, Methodology of Research in Education, Sterling publishers pvt. Ltd.

Internet sources -
www.google.com
Www.Shodhganga.Com

CHAPTER SEVEN

Incorporation of Digital Technology in Teaching

Papai Mondal

Ph.D. Research Scholar, Dept. of Education,The University of Burdwan

Abstract:

Digital technology has affected almost every aspect of life today, and teaching-learning is no exception. Digital technologies such as ICT based (e.g., mobile phone, tablet, notebook, computer, laptop, smart TV, etc.), social media (e.g., Facebook, YouTube, Blogs, Twitter, LinkedIn, Telegram, WhatsApp web, etc.), and Programmed Learning (online courses, e.g., Swayam, Swayam Prabha, MOOC, etc.) have become increasingly popular in recent years. All schools, colleges, and universities today are focusing more on digital education. Especially since the time of Covid-19, the demand for this technology-based education has been strong. Online courses now have more demand than traditional face-to-face courses. The online platform is available 24×7, so students can participate at their convenient time, as they are not bound by a specific and strict schedule. This online education is easily accessible on various devices that are easily known to all the students and are eco-friendly. The government is also taking a positive attitude towards technology-based education and taking various initiatives, as a result of which this education is reaching even the remote villages today. Online education is a growing face of India's education system. Since the new Education Policy (NEP) in 2020, many changes have been made in the education system, including online education.

Keywords: Digital Technology, Eco-friendly, Online Courses, Teaching-Learning, Traditional Course.

1. Introduction:

During the last two decades, the world has undergone a massive revolution with the increasing impact of technology in our lives.

Technology has permeated every part of our lives right from our consumer behavior to our communication medium. Industries too have thrived in this changing situation while having to adapt quickly to meet the evolving lifestyle necessities.

It is no astonishment then that technology has pervaded the education sector and has proclaimed its presence in it. A field that has the most impact on individuals in particular and society in general education is in terrible need of some revolution. Various aspects of education like learning management, content management, etc. have altered with the use of technology. Descriptive examinations have been best rated as assessments that can measure learning outcomes best in the possible circumstances. The possibility of delays and errors has been a perennial challenge in the successful administration of a descriptive examination on a large scale.

The University of Cambridge first tested digital evaluation for the Local Examinations Syndicate in 1999. It was then adopted as a best practice in 2004. In India, the Central Board of Secondary Education (CBSE) set the ball rolling for the faster espousal of this technology in the country. At present, this system of evaluation is being used by various educational institutions around the world.

Technology is the application of scientific knowledge about learning and the conditions of learning to improve the effectiveness and competence of teaching and learning. When the whole country was under lockdown for Covid-19, e-learning was the best and only alternative for students to learn. At present time, technology is playing a vital role in every aspect of human life. According to the current situation, India has reached the highest place in the field of education. Digitalization is forward-moving in the education system of India and is replacing the conventional classroom practice. Educational Technology in the field of study investigates the process of analyzing, designing, developing, implementing, and evaluating the instructional environment, learning materials, learners, and the learning process to improve teaching and learning. Education technology is primarily considered a combination of two interpretations, such as-

1. Technology in Education / Hardware aspects of Education/ICT-based Education &
2. Technology of Education/ Software aspects of Education/ Programmed Learning.

The technology in education concept refers to presenting information in all possible ways. All educational and training gadgets, such as TVs, language test equipment, and various project equipment, including all audio-visual aids. Overhead projectors, video cassette recorders, tape recorders, TV monitors, Microcomputers, etc. Technology in Education is also known as the approach of hardware aspects in education, in the present scenario which is also known as ICT-based education. In the context of ICT-based education, online teaching-learning has been introduced instead of teaching and learning in traditional classrooms. Online classes (Zoom, Skype, Google Classroom, Meet, etc.), online exams, and online assessments (Quizziz, Hot Potatoes, Testomoz, etc.) are also introduced by theICT-based education.

In the other context Technology of Education is closely associated with the modern principles of programmed learning and is characterized by task analysis, writing precise objectives, selection of appropriate learning strategies, reinforcement of correct responses, and constant evaluation, and also online courses, credit-based achievement, etc. Programmed learning is an educational technique characterized by self-paced, self-administered instruction presented in a logical sequence and with many repetitions of concepts and there is no fixed time interval for learning. Students may learn at their own pace. Learning by doing maxim of teaching is followed to involve learners in the learning process. Students are exposed only to correct responses, therefore, the possibility to commit errors is reduced.

The Government of India launched the 'Digital India' initiative in July 2015, to strengthen online infrastructure and expand Internet access among citizens (for example, connecting rural areas to high-speed Internet networks). As part of the 'Digital India' initiative, the government has also launched e-learning initiatives to provide online education in remote and urban areas using smartphones, apps, and internet services and has also taken so many initiatives to promote online education. In specially, the new education policy (NEP 2020) also recommends various initiatives for digital learning, such as Pilot studies for digital education, the creation of Digital infrastructure, Virtual Labs, Availability of Courses in Different languages by synchronous and asynchronous media, Online Assessments and Examination, Digital repository, Content creation, and Dissemination, etc.

2. Objectives of the study

The main objectives of this study are as under-

i. To understand the Historical development of digital technology;

ii. To understand the impact of Technology in Education and Technology of Education in teaching

iii. To understand the Benefits of Technology in Teaching;

iv. To understand the challenges of Technology in Teaching.

3. Research Methodology:

As per the requirements of the study, descriptive nature is being adopted in the research design. Secondary sources and published articles were extensively used for the collection of data. Distinctively used sources were various web articles.

4. Data Collection:

The research paper depends upon the secondary source of information. To prepare the research paper, the required data is extensively used, as it is descriptive.

5. Discussions:

5.1: Objectives no-1:The Historical Development of Digital technology

1947-1979 -The transistor, which was presented in 1947, paved the way for the development of advanced digital computers. The government, military, and other organizations made use of computer systems throughout the 1950s and 1960s. This research ultimately led to the creation of the World Wide Web.

The 1980s - The 1980s brought computer development to films, robots to industry, and automated teller machines (ATMs) to banks. The computer converted into a familiar machine and by the end of the decade, being able to use one became a stipulation for many jobs. The first cell phone was also introduced during this decade.

The 1990s - By 1992, the World Wide Web had been introduced, and by 1996 the Internet became a usual part of most commercial operations. By the late 1990s, the Internet turns out to be a part of everyday life for almost half of the American population. Analog mobile phones finished way to digital mobile phones in 1991 and the petition soared.

The 2000s - By this decade, the Digital Revolution had commenced spreading all over the developing world; mobile phones were regularly seen, the number of Internet users continued to grow, and the television started to convert from using analog to digital signals. When the 21st century commenced, cell phones were a shared possession and high-definition television converted the most common broadcasting method, substituting analog Television. First introduced in 2003, Myspace, Facebook (2004), and Twitter (2007) altered the world of the announcement, business, and the area of knowledge. Furthermore, the incorporation of various technologies and their historical enlargement helps to demonstrate a new direction in our lives. In terms of data storage, the ability to store data has grown exponentially with terabyte storage now being very manageable.

2010 and beyond - By this decade, the Internet makes up supplementary than 25 percent of the world's population. Mobile communication has to become very important, as approximately 70 percent of the world's population owns a mobile phone. The construction between Internet websites and mobile gadgets has become a standard in communication. It is predicted that by 2015, the innovation of tablet computers will far better personal computers with the use of the Internet and the promise of cloud computing services. This will allow users to devour media and use business applications on their mobile devices, applications that would otherwise be too much for such devices to handle.

5.1.2 Objectives no-II:The impact of Technology in Education and Technology of Education in teaching

Many areas in the education sector are extremely affected by the use of digital technology which is as follows:

Motion pictures, tape recorders, television, teaching machines, and computers are called educational hardware. Due to digitalization, learners'(students) access the Internet effectively and rapidly as it encourages them to work better with the scholastic exercises additionally Hardware approach mechanizes the process of teaching so that teachers would be able to deal with more students with fewer expenditures in educating them.

Digitalization assists with setting up e-libraries, classrooms, etc. by giving PC lab, Interactive Whiteboards, (interactive whiteboard or interactive touchscreen) is a display, often with similar measurements to a traditional whiteboard, connected to a computer and a projector.

Virtual Reality Headsets, 3D Printing, Podcasts, etc. in schools, colleges, and universities, as customary libraries are obsolete. It assists with killing obstacles emerging in the method of research exercises.

By giving computers in all study halls educators empower learners to adapt carefully to grammatical mistakes, corrections in spelling, and so forth. It makes exactness in the field of training climate.

In the time of digitalization, learners will in general select through remote courses called correspondence courses at school and colleges. Learners can get course structure and details through mail. Appreciative of innovation for effective availability towards the enrolment for different courses at a particular level.

In another term Software Approach is concerned with teaching objectives in behavioral terms, principles of teaching, methods of teaching, reinforcement of instructional system, feedback, reviews, and evaluation. The software approach tries to develop all the three basic components of technology, i.e., Input, Process, and Output.

In the context of Software approach the online so many programs were run equally with traditional education. The online platform is available 24 × 7, so students can participate at their convenient time, as they are not bound by a specific and strict schedule. These programs are as under-

UGC-MOOC

UGC MOOCs- A vertical of Study Webs of Active–Learning for Young Aspiring Minds (SWAYAM) portal, UGC has launched MOOC initiated by the govt. of India to enable access, equity, and quality within the domain of education for the aspirants. MOOCs provide an affordable and flexible way to learn new skills, advance your career and deliver quality educational involvements at scale. MOOCs validate an informal learning model. Most people enrolled in MOOCs are not college students seeking a degree, but rather students looking for personal enrichment and lifelong learning opportunities.

e-Pathya

e-Pathya (Offline Access) is another vertical of e-Pathshala, a software-driven course/content package that helps students pursue education (PG level) through distance learning yet as a campus learning mode. This vertical also allows offline access to course content. It provides access to digital textbooks for all classes, and graded learning materials and enables participation in exhibitions, contests, festivals, workshops, etc. Students, Teachers, Educators, and Parents can access eBooks through multiple technology podiums that as mobile phones and tablets (as epub) and from the web through laptops and desktops (such as Flipbook). e-pathshala also permits users to carry as numerous books as their device supports. Features of these books consent users to pinch, select, zoom, bookmark, highlight, navigate, share and make notes digitally. At Present ePathshala mobile app is obtainable and complete an especially developed mobile app interface on Android, iOS, and Windows platforms for broader access. It contains textbooks and other e-books such as E-Pub 3.0 and Flipbooks in English, Hindi, and Urdu.

Shodhganga platform

in June 2009, The Shodhganga@INFLIBNET Centre provides a platform for research students to deposit their Ph.D. theses and make them available to the entire scholarly community in open access. The repository has the power to capture, index, store, broadcast, and preserve ETDs submitted by the researchers. As per the Regulation, the responsibility of hosting, maintaining, and making the digital repository of Indian Electronic Theses and Dissertation (called 'Shodhganga'), accessible to all organizations and universities, is assigned to the INFLIBNET Centre by UGC. Shodhganga stands for the reservoir of Indian intellectual output stored in a repository hosted and maintained by the INFLIBNET Centre. Shodhganga replicates the academic structure of each University in terms of Departments / Centres and Colleges each University has to facilitate ease of navigation. The structure also facilitates research scholars from universities to deposit their theses in the respective Department / Centre / College.

e-Shodh Sindhu platform

e-Shodh Sindhu was formed with the merger of three consortia, namely UGC-INFONET Digital Library Consortium, NLIST, and INDEST-AICTE Consortium in December 2015. The most objective of the e-Shodh Sindhu: Consortia for instruction E-Resources is to supply access to qualitative electronic resources including full-text, bibliographic and factual databases to academic institutions at a lower rate of subscription. E-ShodhSindhu consortium is the backbone of research in the higher education system in India. E-ShodhSindhu consortium provides full text and bibliographical journal databases to higher education institutions at a subscription cost.

PM eVIDYA Programme

The e-Vidya program began in May 2020 in response to the COVID-19 pandemic. The Pradhan Mantri eVidya is an initiative by the Ministry of Education that will help facilitate access to digital/online learning and teaching materials of various types among students and teachers. The finance minister also mentioned that the Sawyam Prabha DTH channel would support students who do not have access to the internet. Along with the 'Diksha', an e-content and QR embedded book for all classes, the PM eVidya scheme also has the following programs: For those studying in the 12th grade, a TV channel called 12th One Class was launched. The government would also ensure that visually and hearing-impaired students are accommodated by making specialized e-content and radio broadcasts. The government carried out these efforts so that there would be no impact on the education of students when the countrywide lockdown was imposed.

DIKSHA

In September 2017, the government introduced DIKSHA. DIKSHA is an initiative of the National Council of Educational Research and Training (NCERT) under the aegis of the Ministry of Education, Government of India. DIKSHA is a unique initiative that leverages existing highly scalable and flexible digital infrastructures while keeping teachers at the center. It is built considering the whole teacher's life cycle - from the time student teachers enroll in Teacher Education Institutes (TEIs) to after they retire as teachers. DIKSHA can be accessed free of cost by anyone. It also offers more than 100 microservices as building blocks for the development of platforms and solutions. It is designed to support multiple languages and solutions. At present, it supports 18+ languages and various curricula of NCERT, CBSE, and SCERT pan India.

SWAYAM

WAYAM is a program initiated by the Government of India in 2017 and designed to achieve the three cardinal principles of Education Policy viz., access, equity, and quality. This effort to take the best teaching-learning resources to all, including the most disadvantaged. SWAYAM seeks to bridge the digital divide for students who have hitherto remained untouched by the digital revolution and have not been able to join the mainstream of the knowledge economy.

SWAYAM PRABHA

In 2017, The SWAYAM PRABHA is a group of 22 DTH channels devoted to telecasting high-quality educational programs on a 24X7 basis using the GSAT-15 satellite. It has curriculum-based course content covering diverse disciplines. This is primarily aimed at making quality learning resources accessible to remote areas where internet availability is still a challenge. The SWAYAM PRABHA has new content every day for at least (4) hours which would be repeated 5 more times in a day, allowing the students to choose the time of their convenience. The channels are uplinked from BISAG, Gandhinagar. The contents are provided by NPTEL, IITs, UGC, CEC, IGNOU, NCERT, and NIOS. The INFLIBNET Centre maintains the web portal.

NISHTHA

The Department of School Education and Literacy has launched a National Mission to improve learning outcomes at the elementary level through an Integrated Teacher Training Programme called NISHTHA under the Centrally Sponsored Scheme of Samagra Shiksha in 2019-20. NISHTHA is a capacity-building program for "Improving Quality of School Education through Integrated Teacher Training". It aims to build competencies among all the teachers and school principals at the elementary stage. NISHTHA is the world's largest teachers' training program of its kind. The basic objective of this massive training program is to motivate and equip teachers to encourage and foster critical thinking in students. The initiative is the first of its kind wherein standardized training modules are developed at the national level for all States and UTs.

The above discussion clearly states that the impact of digital technology in teaching is very useful to our learners as well as our teachers. Technology can help educators create blended learning environments and leverage digital tools for formative and summative assessments, bringing new models for learning and teaching to classrooms.

5.1.3 Objectives no-III:The Benefits of Technology in Teaching

Teachers want to improve student performance, and technology can help them accomplish this aim. To mitigate the challenges, administrators should help teachers gain the competencies needed to enhance learning for students through technology. The benefits of technology in teaching are discussed in the following.

Increased Collaboration and Communication

The biggest impact that technology has made on collaboration is the way teams communicate with each other. It's much easier to schedule meetings and calls thanks to applications that allow team members to share their calendars and schedules with each other. Technology enables one-on-one interaction with teachers. Students can ask classroom-related questions and seek additional help with a difficult understanding of the subject matter and the result is increased collaboration and communication with students and teachers in the classroom and outside the classroom. Common examples include Internet forums (also known as discussion boards or message boards), which serve as a discussion platform on the Internet to facilitate as well as manage online messages. online chat, which is a discussion platform online that facilitates as well as manages real-time messages. instant messaging.

Personalized Learning Opportunities

Personalized learning is an educational approach that aims to customize learning for each student's strengths, needs, skills, and interests. Each student gets a learning plan that's based on what they know and how they learn best. Personalized learning makes students intrinsically motivated to learn. Instead of being told what to learn, they can choose their own path out of a set of options. Because what they choose is personally meaningful to them, they have intrinsic motivation to succeed. Just like that, the online platform is available 24 × 7, so students can participate at their convenient time, as they are not bound by a specific and strict schedule.

Curiosity Driven by Engaging Content

Curiosity-driven behavior is often defined as behavior through which knowledge is gained, and therefore encompasses all behaviors that provide access to or increase sensory information. Through engaging and educational content, teachers can spark inquisitiveness in children and boost their curiosity, which research says has ties to academic success. Curiosity helps students get a better understanding of math and reading concepts.

Improved Teacher Productivity and Efficiency

Teachers can leverage technology to achieve new levels of productivity, implement Teachers implement useful digital tools to expand learning opportunities for students, and increase student useful student support and engagement. It interacts with students and teachers and gives them a personal touch, creating interest that is missing in the traditional ways of learning. In the process of making the teacher's work easier, involving students can boost the productivity and creativity of teachers and learners. Technology helps a teacher in improving teaching with the use of AV (audiovisual) recording. It is learning equipment that maximizes learning with the help of auditory and visual systems including LCD Projector, TV, computer, video, etc.

Become a Leader in Enriching Classrooms through Technology

Courses such as Education Program and Policy Implementation and Teaching Science in Elementary School equip graduate students with critical competencies to incorporate technology into educational settings effectively.

Some perspectives of technical teaching in education are not confined to small boundaries. The benefits of digital technology in teaching are not a narrow term, its aspects are broad. With more and more people getting into digital media, it is essential for teachers to use the latest tools available in their work to engage students. To engage students in learning, one needs to be innovative and new ideas should be introduced so that students get excited about what they are learning.

5.1.4 Objectives no-IV:Challenges of technology in teaching

Relevant research has proven that technology could change education negatively through four paths: deteriorating students' competencies of reading and writing, dehumanizing educational environments, distorting social interactions between teachers and students, and isolating individuals when using technology. The disadvantages of technology in teaching are as-

Learning Is Becoming More Expensive

With the widespread use of technology, it is becoming increasingly expensive. As a result, many people stay away from its use. Here the question arises why it's becoming more expensive? There are so many reasons, such as there is a difference between new tech and a brand or model. Industrial competition results in a marketing cycle where the product goes from new and expensive to a commodity. The technology-rich brand of an organization and its advertisement attract our attention, but the cost of all this has to be borne by the students and others of that organization. Apart from these, some of the technologies used in education are really expensive. As a result, learning is costly.

Insufficient Teaching Methods

Teaching is Insufficient; Learning is also Insufficient. In the field of education, there is a dearth of suitable teaching methods for teaching through technology. This lack prevents students from learning through technology. The lack of training and adaptation of teachers to the use of technology in the classroom affects their ability to make the most of these new technological opportunities.

Misguiding & Misuse of Information

Misguiding of information leads the students in another direction. It is all about making bad use of information technology for personal interest or in order to create a troublesome situation for others. Plagiarism is one aspect. It is passing off the work of other people as your own without giving any credit to them. A negative aspect of technology, it's helping students and others to cheat easily in any type of circumstance. So, all these are the misuse of technology.

Extra Distractions for Students

Various studies have shown that nearly Half of Students are distracted by technology there are so many unnecessary advertisements, and programs that distract the students, that the students are badly affected. Top distractions for students include social media, texting, television, and family, which can pull one's attention away from the task at hand and diminish productivity. Apart from these, competing priorities, ubiquitous technology, and the daily pressures of school and social life contribute to the many distractions students face while learning.

Technology Sometimes Fails

There are many reasons our technology may not deliver the performance or functionality we require. Poor implementation, inadequate maintenance, a lack of I.T. resource capacity, the complexity of modern solutions, and misaligning systems to business requirements are just some of the causes. Sometimes technology's flaws make it difficult for students to learn. This is because at other times students are unable to fill the knowledge gap in that particular situation.

There are also some other disadvantages, such as Misleading and misguiding information, the Risk of cyber-attacks and hacks, the risk to the traditional book and handwriting methods, implementing computers and the internet for ICT replace the convention education curriculums, managing courses online is difficult, Misuse of technology, etc.

6. Conclusion:

Overall, a study on the effect of computing and emerging technology on teaching-learning consistently find favorable outcomes. Apart from teaching, there is a touch of technology in every aspect of human life today. Today society is constantly changing. This variability is the law of nature. Due to the change in the flow of this rule, people have adopted this technology today. Technology has taken place in every corner of society today. Today technology is giving a chance backward student to move forward today. The positive steps taken by the Government of India have made the education system for students easier. This study will be very informative to the readers. Analysis of secondary information will influence the reader's mind toward technology-based learning. The progress of society is not a mere measure. Proper use of technology symbolizes the progress of society.

References:

Al-Bataineh, A., Harris, J. L., & Al-Bataineh, M. T. (2016). One to One Technology and its Effect on Student Academic Achievement and Motivation. *Contemporary Educational Technology, 7*(4). https://doi.org/10.30935/cedtech/6182

Clark-Wilson, A., Robutti, O., & Thomas, M. (2020). Teaching with digital technology. *ZDM, 52*(7), 1223–1242. https://doi.org/10.1007/s11858-020-01196-0

Deepthi, T. (2021). A Paradigm Shift through Digital Technology in Teaching and Learning Process. *International Journal of Advanced Research in Science, Communication, and Technology*, 100–103. https://doi.org/10.48175/ijarsct-v2-i3-317

Greve, K., & Tan, A. (2021). Reimagining the role of technology in higher education: the new normal and learners' likes. *Compass: Journal of Learning and Teaching*, *14*(3). https://doi.org/10.21100/compass.v14i3.1231

Gurukkal, R. (2021). Future Higher Education. *Higher Education for the Future*, *9*(1), 7. https://doi.org/10.1177/23476311211063698

Kalolo, J. F. (2018). Digital revolution and its impact on education systems in developing countries. *Education and Information Technologies*, *24*(1), 345–358. https://doi.org/10.1007/s10639-018-9778-3

Mridul Mazumdar @Mridul Mazumdar May 27, 2020, 18:51 IST. (2020, May 27). *The history and usefulness of online teaching in India.* Times of India Blog. https://timesofindia.indiatimes.com/readersblog/mridul-mazumdar/the-history-and-usefulness-of-online-teaching-in-india-20481/

Nadeem, A., Malik, N., & Noreen, S. (2021). Learning Management System: An Innovation in Teaching Learning Process at University Level. *Journal of Entrepreneurship, Management, and Innovation*, *3*(2), 409–428. https://doi.org/10.52633/jemi.v3i2.106

Olofsson, A. D., Fransson, G., & Lindberg, J. O. (2019). A study of the use of digital technology and its conditions with a view to understandingaims what 'adequate digital competence' may mean in a national policy initiative. *Educational Studies*, *46*(6), 727–743. https://doi.org/10.1080/03055698.2019.1651694

Pritam, B. P. (2022). Blended Teaching and Learning in Teacher Education Sector in India: Present and Future Prospects. *SSRN Electronic Journal.* https://doi.org/10.2139/ssrn.4027445

Mental Health of Children: A Post-Pandemic Challenging Issue Highlighting Education

Parnab Ghosh

Assistant Professor,Department of Education,Panskura Banamali College (Autonomous),Purba Medinipur, West Bengal.

Abstract

COVID-19 has had a significant impact on our lives. Learning healthy ways to deal with stress can help you become more resilient. Every aspect of life has been affected by the pandemic. It could be in the service, agricultural, or industrial sectors, as well as any other, organized or unorganized sector including the educational sector. Many people, even children, have likely encountered stress, worry, fear, sadness, and loneliness, leading to mental health issues, including anxiety, and depression. For around two and a half years, schools were shuttered. Many children maintained their education through E-Learning; however, many school-aged youngsters were forced to drop out due to a lack of technical gadgets due to their parents' financial difficulty. Children who have access to E-Learning have become accustomed to online or virtual classrooms and activities; nonetheless, they have become anxious as a result of being isolated from their peers, teachers, and everyday classroom activities. As a result, they have become accustomed to the E-Learning system and are seeking coping mechanisms to alleviate their stress and despair. Although strict constraints have been lifted and educational institutions have embarked on a new path in the post-pandemic period, the children have yet to recover from the effects of such stress. This qualitative study has identified several major difficulties with children's mental health and offered some preventive actions based on secondary data to address children's mental health issues, which have become a difficult issue in the post-pandemic period.

Keywords: Pandemic, Educational Sector, Loneliness, Anxiety, Depression, E-Learning, Virtual Classroom

Introduction

The pandemic of COVID-19 has had a significant impact on our lives. Learning to cope with stress healthily may be very helpful to become more resilient. The pandemic has had a great impact on every sphere of life. It may be the service sector, agricultural and industrial sectors, any kind of organized and unorganized sector as well as the educational sector. A lot of people including children might have experienced stress, anxiety, fear, sadness, and loneliness which resulted in mental health disorders, anxiety, and depression. Schools were closed for around two and a half years. A great number of children continued their studies through E-Learning but at the same time, many school-goer children were out of the study due to the non-availability of technical devices for the financial crisis of their parents. The children who got the facility of E-Learning have been habituated with the online or virtual classes and activities, they also become stressed from being isolated from their friends, teachers, and daily classroom activities. Consequently, they have become mechanical with the E-Learning system and are looking for coping strategies to get rid of that stress and depression. Though stringent rules have been withdrawn and educational institutions have started a new journey in this post-pandemic period but the children could not get over the sickness of such stress yet. This qualitative study has pointed out some serious issues regarding the mental health of children and suggested some preventive measures by collecting data from some secondary sources to overcome the problems of children's mental health which becomes a challenging issue in the post-pandemic period.

The Backdrop

The increase in stress and mental injury is the areas where children and young people attend a change in basic behaviour from pandemic and locking. Children inside, children meet encounters closer to social stress and grief. Many children and young people in India, who lost their main or secondary caregivers to Coronavirus, found themselves without emotional support. In addition, for more than a year, children and youth have come into contact with digital pedagogy. A strong increase in e-Learning platforms, because of the appearance of the Covid19 pandemic, not only changing global learning, but also the way students communicate with their colleagues and with the family environment. For many of them, the pandemic has taken away the opportunity to experience important milestones in their lives, such as graduation, the first day of college or leaving, and more. Psychosocial learning, an important aspect of raising a child, is, unfortunately, a big gap in the absence of a direct school.

Pandemic and Its Impact on Mental Health

Experts believe that children's social isolation, overexposure to social media, and lack of peer support can cause serious mental health problems. These challenges are more acute for children from vulnerable social groups and low-income families, especially those with difficult parenting situations. If left unaddressed, these factors can lead to serious cases of anxiety, depression, and even substance abuse in young people.

Mental Health Issues in the UK

A UK charity has highlighted the impact of coronavirus on the mental health of schoolchildren in the UK. The UK is one of the countries affected by a coronavirus in Europe. Lockdown measures in the UK were announced on 23 March 2020 and resulted in the closure of schools and businesses. Parents and students have been instructed to stay home and isolate themselves from the outside world to limit the spread of the virus. The effects of incarceration, more than two months after being incarcerated, are beginning to be felt. The slowing economy, layoffs, job losses, and the work-from-home policy have had a huge impact on adults in the UK. The impact of coronavirus on mental health, however, is the mental health impact the coronavirus pandemic is having on children that have alarmed the UK's largest charity group, Barnardo's. They point out that these children have been isolated from the outside world, their social environment is briefly destroyed, and their safe space is in school. According to Barnardo, the mental health damage caused by closures requires special attention when schools finally reopen. They went on to suggest that if the mental impact of the coronavirus on these youngsters is not addressed when schools reopen, it will be a missed opportunity. They also emphasize those vulnerable children are more susceptible to the epidemic and require special attention.

Indian Perspectives

A recent report by The Lancet titled "COVID19 and Adolescent Mental Health in India" shares some important notes on how India can create a framework for early detection of threats to mental health in this age group. Teachers and parents can be taught to recognize indications and symptoms of mental illness, such as trouble sleeping, excessive anger, and difficulties in concentrating, according to the report. Mental health practitioners also suggest developing an elaborate, evidence-based action plan that can address the emotional and psychological needs of young people in this time of crisis. Recognizing the urgency of this crisis, the Indian government has launched a series of programmes including the KIRAN mental health rehabilitation hotline for early detection and diagnosis of mental health disorders among adolescents.

The Initiative of UNICEF

UNICEF (United Nations International Children's Emergency Fund) has urged more investment in Mental Health and Psychosocial Support Services (MHPSS) for children, particularly in poor and middle-income countries, on World Mental Health Day (10 October 2020).

UNICEF promotes family-centered support, as well as developing healthy family relationships, caregiver engagement, and greater investment in schools and communities, to ensure that all children, especially those who are experiencing difficulties at home can feel safe, connected, and tranquil. UNICEF also advocates for increased investment in MHPSS during humanitarian crises, as well as increased focus on protecting children from the detrimental impacts of the digital world on their mental health.

Now is the time to break the silence and mobilize political will and public support to invest in mental health and the best possible psychosocial outcomes from infancy through adulthood.

Psychological Observations and Recommendations

Psychologist Descartes's Point of View

On November 10, developmental psychologist Christine Descartes said that the mental health issues that are developing in children and adolescents as a result of e-learning have created a second pandemic at a virtual panel discussion hosted by UWI in collaboration with the United Nations Educational, Scientific, and Cultural Organization (UNESCO) in honour of World Science Day. She further said that Covid19 had brought in a second epidemic, this time one of fear, anxiety, and other mental health issues. Confinement and isolation, according to Descartes, have been shown to increase stress levels, and social distancing techniques, while important, have negative effects similar to medications. She also mentioned that psychologists have found a "bidirectional" effect, in which mental health concerns might prevent people from learning in a virtual environment in certain cases, while virtual learning can lead to mental health problems in others.

According to Descartes, children who are bullied at school or socially alienated in a face-to-face environment, are thriving in the virtual classroom recently, because they are not distracted by the burden of dealing with bullies regularly. However, the predominance of death fear can block students' focus in some situations, she noted. Children are worried about their mortality as well as the mortality of their loved ones.

She claims that adolescent mental health problems are more common because of a lack of social connection, especially for students between ten and nineteen. Adolescents require a lot more interaction because it is vital for their cognitive and social development.

Role of teachers

Collaborative exercises, regular conversations, and the use of technology to provide alternate communication channels should all be used by teachers to build a feeling of community.

The three main roles of a teacher are-

• Creating digitally collaborative mini-workouts regularly. In the digital environment, regular communication with various co-workers fosters a sense of community.

• Encouraging students to look through course materials in virtual study groups in online discussion forums. Learners can freshen up misunderstandings, demonstrate their understanding, and more effectively remember data by discussing course material.

• Improving communication between co-workers and instructors, software such as video chat platforms and even virtual reality applications could be leveraged. In collaborative tasks, this is very useful. Teachers can also offer regular "working hours" when students can interact with them in a "live" digital environment and discuss the course material.

Conclusion

Given the current crisis, several key questions have been identified such as, can mental health problems caused by overexposure to technology be limited by an integrated pedagogical approach? What support systems and helpline frameworks need to be institutionalized for early detection and broader coverage of mental health diagnoses? How can parents and family members be better trained to support children and young people during this time? Are schools and educational institutions in India well equipped to meet the mental health needs of students after they continue their face-to-face studies? Are social media platforms investing in mental health awareness and existing support mechanisms? All these questions are still seeking answers and we have to keep patience to get the answers for the time being.

Web Sources

Children's mental health should be a priority post-pandemic, A UK campaigners say | English Forward (englishforums.com)

https://www.englishforums.com/news/uk-children-mental-health-post-pandemic/?msclkid=3ce52491bcc011ec91deb7fb81885902

The time for a child mental health revolution is now - UNICEF Connect

Psychologist: Mental health is second pandemic (Newsday.co.tt)

https://pubmed.ncbi.nlm.nih.gov/34260295

https://www.ncbi.nlm.nih.gov/pmc/articles/PMC8457633

https://theboar.org/2020/11/how-will-online-learning-impact-student...

3 Common eLearning Health Issues And How To Overcome Them - eLearning Industry

Assessing the Presence of Techno-pedagogical Skills among the Trainee Teacher Educators

Adrija Chattopadhyay

Assistant Professor, Dr. B. R. Ambedkar Institute of Education & Research Scholar, Department of Education, Adamas University

Abstract: Technology, the most important and inseparable part of present scenario has left its marks on education also. Side by side the knowledge of Pedagogy, technological knowledge also becomes important for the teachers. So to equip the trainee teachers with such knowledge the teacher educators have to be equipped with the technological concepts. In this research paper the researcher wanted to find out the presence of techno-pedagogical knowledge between the Science and Arts stream teacher educators, male and female as well as urban and rural teacher educators. The result of the quantitative research revealed that there was no difference in the presence of the techno-pedagogical skills between the Arts and Science stream teacher educators and also between the male and female teacher educators. The Urban teacher educators had higher level of techno-pedagogical knowledge than the rural teacher educators.

Keywords: Assessing, Presence, Techno-pedagogical, Trainee Teacher educators

INTRODUCTION:

Civilization changes or can be said developed with the passage of time. As time flows changes have become inevitable. Whatever was fiction in earlier times has become reality nowadays. In this age of Digitalization and Globalization we are successful in reaching to the land of Moon, we can buy land there, robots and rockets have become the normal phenomena of our everyday life. When we are under the umbrella of technology, one of the most inseparable factors of our lives, education also gets benefitted by the implementation of technology as well. Nowadays the blackboards have become smart boards, chalks have changed into markers, audio- visual machines which were once thought to be a luxury good, have become now the most essential thing of teaching learning process. 'Technology permits all walks of life and most every field of human endeavor and technological skills are becoming essential for all subject areas because the acquisition and dissemination of information in all fields.' (Anand, 2019).The advent of covid 19 has reminded us the importance of laptop and smart phones. Once every guardian who complained about the addiction towards mobile phone of his/her ward, now is handing over to him a costly smart phone to keep the light of knowledge abroad. Pedagogy is a term associated with teaching. It refers to the arts and Science of teaching. So to become a successful teacher one should have proper knowledge of pedagogy. Except the bookish knowledge a teacher should know the child psychology, curriculum, innovative teaching learning process. In addition to this, here added the knowledge of technology. To become a smart teacher in this smart world one should have a proper knowledge of mingling the pedagogical knowledge with technological knowledge to make the class vibrant, interactive and lively. 'Techno-pedagogy refers to electronically mediated courses that integrate sound pedagogic principles of teaching and learning with the use of technology. The Techno Pedagogy Knowledge collaboratively developed frame work of scholars and researchers seeking to conceptualize and clarify the competencies that evolve from the intersection between pedagogy and technology.' (Prakash & Hooda, 2017). Techno Pedagogical Content Knowledge known as TPACK (developed by Shulman) has become the key component of present day teaching learning process. To nourish the teachers with such advance knowledge of teaching the teacher educators should first have the particular technological knowledge. To meet the demand of the present 21st century education system, the teacher educators should be equipped with such skills so that they can easily teach and transfer such skills to the teacher trainees or to the would be teachers so that in the future course of time they can be a great advisor to the backbone of our nations, the school going children.

REVIEW OF RELATED LITERATURE:

Thakur, N. (2015). in his article discussed about the need of techno-pedagogical skills in the modern world. ICT can be used to demystify the work of the scientists and can act as a link between the students and the scientist. So to make all the students computer literate it is essential for all the teachers to learn the technology based pedagogical skills as their teaching based on these skills can lead the future generation towards ultimate success. The barriers for implementing the techno-pedagogical skills were conversed here and the probable measures to minimize the problems were also discussed here as the result of the study. Enhancement of the knowledge of English, paying incentives to the teachers, different programs based on techno-pedagogical services, co-ordination among various departments, and development of techno-pedagogical electronic content can be used as the arms to fight with such challenges. Hanane, L. & Djilali, B. (2015). in their research study discussed about the importance of ICT skills for both the students and the teachers. In this particular research the researchers took 240 Algerian University Teachers as sample and through survey method. They tried to discuss the importance of ICT in education and how ICT can be a great help for the development of techno-pedagogical skills among the teachers and the learners. As the result of the study it was revealed that the technological difficulties and attachment of the teachers to the old teaching learning process were creating the barriers. In recommendations, they advised to bridge the gap in between technology and pedagogy. There should be various software skill training programs for the teachers and also a standard for professional skill should be maintained. M, Leema & Saleem, M. (2017). in their research paper analyzed the various areas of curriculum of teacher education and the infusion of techno-pedagogic skills into it. Content Analysis was done as methodology. This technological skill not only has a positive effect on the teachers but also it has a severe effect on the knowledge of the students. Though some aspects of techno-pedagogical skills were included in the curriculum of elementary education, there were certain areas where the gap remained the same. In this paper the researchers found out the gap in the curriculum side by side they also provided suggestions for their future improvement. There were not any specific education and also awareness of the elementary course in the government sector. In the private sector the condition was more horrible. Some courses based on ICT should be introduced in in-service teachers training. High quality ICT based quality resource, academic books based on ICT, initiation and motivations for ICT integration were given as recommendation. Bala, P. (2018). in her descriptive survey based research study wanted to find out the Techno-pedagogical competence and anxiety of using teaching aids in the classroom of the 100 senior secondary school teachers of both the Government and the Private Schools by stratified random sampling. Percentage, t test, standard deviation and regression were used as statistical techniques. Most of the senior secondary teachers possessed average and high level of competence in techno-pedagogical area. Most of the teachers showed low level of anxiety towards using instructional aids. There was no significant difference in using teaching aids by the male and female teachers. Sana, et. al. (2018). in their research article wanted to describe the importance of integrating technology with appropriate pedagogical knowledge. Adequate combination of pedagogy and technology can make a teacher apt and successful in his/her professional achievement. 'Process Oriented Skills' helps a learner to combat all hazards in the future time to come. In this paper the researchers wanted to find out the technological skills of the teachers and how these skills were used in a classroom of multi-media context to develop the 'Process Oriented Skills' of the learners. Islam, M. (2020). in his research paper discussed about the importance of techno-pedagogical skills in covid-19 situation. The pandemic reflected the need of technological skills in the present day. This study wanted to discuss the journey of the teachers from pedagogy to techno-pedagogy, the significance of techno-pedagogical skills among the teachers and the challenges in acquiring the skills. Some probable measures of improving the skills were also discussed here. In this research the researchers used various past researches for analysis. The result revealed that use of multi-media, electronic dictionaries, use of computer, blogging, internet text chatting, E-mail writing could be used as the probable solutions of this problem. Nayar, A. & Akmar, S. (2020). in their research paper wanted to evaluate a 'Technology based Teacher Education Course' designed specifically for pre-service science teachers. A 'TPACK Assessment Inventory' was used to analyze if the seven parts of TPACK knowledge were included in the pre-service teacher education program or not and the result revealed the importance of all the seven parts in teacher education equally. So this study suggested some changes as that should be incorporated in pre-service teacher education program to aptly incorporate the TPACK knowledge among the pre-service science teachers. Asad, et. al. (2021). in their research paper discuss about the various innovative strategies used in the 21st century classroom. Though there were various obstacles in implementing technological skills in the classroom, there are various skills and methods through which such innovative practices can be used in the classroom with proper utilization and advantage. The research was done on Arts and Science teachers of Sukkur state Government College and various sources like Google, Science Direct, Google Scholar, Emerald, Springer, Eric databases were used to complete the Mixed Method Research. The result showed that there was no difference in the presence of techno-pedagogical skills between the Arts and Science teachers. Some suggestions were also provided to fulfill the educational needs of the society. Sharma, N. & Sharma, R. (2021). in their research paper discussed about the presence of Techno-pedagogical Skills among the Arts and Science Teachers of Jammu Province. `100 samples were taken and a self-made standardized questionnaire was used in this mixed method research. By analyzing the score through Percentage, Mean, Standard Deviation and t test the result revealed that the Science Stream teacher trainees had higher level of Techno-pedagogical Skills than the arts Stream trainee teachers. This study would be a great help not only for the teacher educators rather it would be helpful for the entire professional for sustaining in 21st century technical world. Thirunavukkarasu, M. (2021). in his research paper investigated the presence of Techno-pedagogical skills among the B.Ed. trainee teachers of Tiruchirapalli District. The research was done as a descriptive one using a normative survey. 'Scale on Techno-pedagogical Skills' was used by the researcher to get the statistical analysis result. The result revealed that the Techno-pedagogical Skills among the trainee teachers were average and there was no difference in the presence of Techno-pedagogical skills in between the urban and rural and also in between the male and female trainee teachers.

STATEMENT OF THE PROBLEM:

The problem of the following study was stated below-

Assessing the Presence of Techno-pedagogical Skills among the Trainee Teacher Educators

OBJECTIVES:

1. To measure the presence of techno-pedagogical skills among the Science and Arts stream based trainee teacher educators.

1. To quantify the difference in the presence of techno-pedagogical skills between the male and female trainee teacher educators.
2. To gauge the contrast in the existence of techno-pedagogical skills between the urban and rural teacher educators.

HYPOTHESIS:

1. There would have been no difference in the presence of Techno-pedagogical Skills among the Science and Arts stream based trainee teacher educators.
2. No difference would have been observed in the presence of techno-pedagogical skills between the male and female trainee teacher educators.
3. There would have been no difference in the presence of Techno-pedagogical Skills among the urban and rural trainee teacher educators.

OPERATIONAL DEFINITION OF THE TERMS:

Assessing- Assessing generally means evaluating or estimating something. Here in this present study assessing refers to the measurement of techno-pedagogical skills among the trainee teacher educators.

Presence- Presence means a thing or a person who actually exists or present in a particular place but he may not be seen. In the present study the existence of techno-pedagogical skills among the trainee teacher educators were measured.

Techno-pedagogical Skills- Pedagogy refers to the arts, science and crafts of teaching. When it is termed as techno-pedagogy, the technological knowledge is associated with pedagogical skills (motivation, teaching learning process and the development of skills)and these are associated with techno-pedagogical aspects like interactive whiteboard, computers, internet etc.

Trainee Teacher educators- Teacher educators are generally the teachers of B.Ed. colleges under whom the B.Ed. trainees are trained. Here the trainee teacher educators mean the M.Ed. students and they were the sample of this study.

DELIMITATIONS:

1. The study was done only with 120 trainee teacher educators.
2. The samples were collected from M.Ed. colleges of Kolkata and Howrah Region.
3. The study could be done in a great scale.
4. Only techno-pedagogical skills of the trainee teacher educators were measured here.

SIGNIFICANCE OF THE PROBLEM:

Pedagogy is regarded as one of the most important aspect of teacher training education. But in the era of 21st century only the methodologies of learning and teaching are not the important criteria rather technological skills must be added with it to cope up with the rat race. The knowledge of combining technology and pedagogy can lead a teacher towards the path of development. To teach the teacher trainees, it is very essential for the teacher educators to be acquainted with such pedagogical skills associated with the skills related to technology. So the M.Ed. students should develop such skills from the very beginning of their training. So in this study the presence of techno-pedagogical skills among the trainee teacher educators was measured to see how much techno-pedagogically efficient they are.

METHODOLOGY:

The research was done based on Descriptive Quantitative Method. Descriptive survey was used for collecting the data. A standardized questionnaire was used to collect the data from the sample. Content Validity of the questionnaire was checked. Reliability was checked through Split-half Method (.91).

VARIABLES:

The Presence of Techno-pedagogical Skills was used here as Dependent variable and the habitat area, age, sex of the trainee teacher educators were used as dependent variable.

POPULATION:

Population of the study consists of all the trainee teacher educators of Kolkata and Howrah region.

SAMPLE:

120 trainee teacher educators were taken here as sample. 60 trainee teacher educators from each area (Kolkata and Howrah) were taken here for the data collection by simple random sampling.

Name of the District	Area	Number of Samples
Howrah	Bally	32
Howrah	Uluberia	28
Kolkata	Saltlake	35
Kolkata	Sonarpur	25

Area	Number of Science Stream based Trainee Teacher Educators	Number of Arts Stream based Trainee Teacher Educators
Bally	14	18
Uliberia	17	11
Saltlake	15	20
Sonarpur	14	11

Area	Number of Male Trainee Teacher Educators	Number of Female Trainee Teacher Educators	Number of Trainee Teacher educators from Village Area	Number of Trainee Teacher educator from Urban Area
Bally	10	22	15	17
Uluberia	15	13	13	15
Saltlake	15	20	20	15
Sonarpur	10	15	15	10

Sample Distribution-

RESEARCH DESIGN:

The research was done based via quantitative method as per the demand of the situation. Descriptive survey was used for collecting the data. A standardized questionnaire was used to collect the data from the sample. Content Validity of the questionnaire was checked by five experts.

Reliability was checked through Test Retest Method (.91). The questionnaire consisted of 42 questions related to the three skills of Techno-pedagogic skills in five point Likert Scale (Always, Sometimes, Undecided, Rarely, Never) was distributed to the samples and the responses were analyzed for finding result. The areas of Techno Pedagogic Skills are as follows- Technological knowledge, Pedagogical knowledge, Technological Pedagogical Knowledge. Each area was covered by 14 questions and thus total 42 questions were completed. Question Number 1,4,6,8,9,10,12,14,16,18,19,21,22,24,25,27,28,30,32,34,35,36,37,39,40 and 41 were done in a positive manner and 2,3,5,7,11,13,15,17,20,23,26,29,31.33,38,42 were done in a negative manner. In the positive statement the marking scheme was 5, 4,3,2,1 but in the negative statement the numbering system was just the opposite.

ANALYSIS AND INTERPRETATION:

HYPOTHESIS-1

There would have been no difference in the presence of Techno-pedagogical Skills among the Science and Arts stream based trainee teacher educators.

Number of Science stream based trainee teacher educators	Mean	Standard Deviation	Number of Arts stream based trainee teacher educators	Mean	Standard Deviation	t value
60	31.23	18.45	60	30.35	17.9	0.2652

For testing the Hypothesis the gained scores of Science and Arts Stream based trainee teacher educators were calculated via Mean, Standard Deviation and t value.

The mean gain score of Science stream based trainee teacher educators was higher than the mean gain score of Arts stream based trainee teacher educator. The t value 0.2652 was lower than the table t value 1.98 at 0.05 level of level of significance at 118 degrees of freedom. Therefore the Hypothesis was accepted and hence it was proved that there would have been no difference in the presence of techno-pedagogical skills between the Science stream based and Arts stream based trainee teacher educators.

HYPOTHESIS-2

No difference would have been observed in the presence of techno-pedagogical skills between the male and female trainee teacher educators.

Number of male trainee teacher educators	Mean	Standard Deviation	Number of female trainee teacher educators	Mean	Standard Deviation	t value
50	25.25	15	70	38.29	18	1.0035

For testing the Hypothesis the gained scores of male and female trainee teacher educators were calculated via Mean, Standard Deviation and t value.

The mean gain score of male trainee teacher educators was lower than the mean gain score of female trainee teacher educator. The t value 1.0035 was lower than the table t value 1.98 at 0.05 level of level of significance at 118 degrees of freedom. Therefore the Hypothesis was accepted and hence it was proved that the no difference would have been observed in the presence of techno-pedagogical skills between the male and female trainee teacher educators.

HYPOTHESIS-3

There would have been no difference in the existence of techno-pedagogical skills between the urban and rural trainee teacher educators.

Number of village trainee teacher educators	Mean	Standard Deviation	Number of rural trainee teacher educators	Mean	Standard Deviation	t value
63	29.20	19	57	38.95	27.25	2.2908

The mean gain score of village trainee teacher educators was lower than the mean gain score of urban trainee teacher educator. The t value 2.2908 was higher than the table t value 1.98 at 0.05 level of level of significance at 118 degrees of freedom. Therefore the Hypothesis was rejected and hence it was proved that there would have been difference in the existence of techno-pedagogical skills between the urban and rural trainee teacher educators.

FINDINGS:

After conducting the whole study some finding were listed below-

1. There would have been no difference in the presence of Techno-pedagogical Skills among the Science and Arts stream based trainee teacher educators.
2. No difference would have been observed in the presence of techno-pedagogical skills between the male and female trainee teacher educators.
3. There would have been difference in the existence of techno-pedagogical skills between the urban and rural trainee teacher educators.
4. In some cases the rural trainee teacher educators may face some difficulties in using the Techno-pedagogical skills if the technical skills are of higher level.
5. In some cases also the Arts stream based trainee teacher educators face some difficulties in using the Techno-pedagogical skills if the technical skills are of higher level.
6. Technology skill enhancing program could be a great help for the development of techno-pedagogical skills.
7. Sometimes the trainee teacher educators could face problem in using the technology in remote areas though they have enough techno-pedagogical skills.
8. In most of the cases more training is needed to integrate the technical as well as pedagogical skills.
9. Sometimes the technological set up in colleges and universities may create problem in applying the skills.
10. The trainee teacher educators need more confidence in applying the skills in classroom.
11. The locality, environment, economic condition might act as variables in the study.

12. More practice and knowledge are needed to be added in the case of implementing techno-pedagogical skills by the trainee teacher educators,

RECOMMENDATIONS AND SUGGESTIONS:

1. The M.Ed. training colleges should be equipped with various technological aids.
2. Some sessions should be arranged by experts from the concerned field to show how technology can be interrelated with pedagogy.
3. Some lecture series could be arranged either offline or in online mode to develop the techno-pedagogical skills of the trainee teacher educators.
4. Techno-pedagogic skills should be introduced from B.Ed. course itself.
5. Various seminars, webinars, conferences, debates, symposium could be arranged for the development of such skills.
6. Some good books should be published and materials should be uploaded online to provide the information related to the Techno-pedagogic skills.
7. In each week training colleges as well as the universities can arrange lecture series/expert opinion session on the use of Techno-pedagogical skills.
8. In rural areas the provision of using technological aids should be increased.
9. Curriculum of M.Ed. course should include Techno-pedagogy in their syllabus.
10. The institution should have UPS or invertors for giving uninterrupted power supply in an institution.
11. Positive attitude among the trainee teacher educators/ trainee teachers should be developed towards the use of Techno-pedagogic skills.
12. There should be co-ordination and support from the end of the staffs as well as from the end of the management personnel.

CONCLUSION:

21st century is an age of digitalization. Technology has become an inevitable part of this generation to sustain the rat race world. To teach the little ones the importance and innovativeness of technology, it is the prime duty of our society to develop them as tech-educated. As school is a place where a child spends most of his time of a day, it is the prime responsibility of a teacher to make them understand the utilization of technology by using the technology himself/ herself. To become a teacher B.Ed. training is of utmost importance. So if they may be aware of the usefulness of technology from their training period it will be easier for them to learn it and use it effectively and innovatively. For this the teacher educators should have proper knowledge of using technical knowledge as well as pedagogical knowledge and the blending of both the strategies to design a teaching learning plan which will be engrossing as well as avant-garde.

REFERENCES:

1. Thakur, N. (2015). *A Study on Implementation of Techno-Pedagogical Skills, Its Challenges and Role to Release at Higher Level of Education.* American International Journal of Research in Humanities, Arts and Social Sciences. pp. 182-186.

2. Hanane, L. & Djilali, B. (2015). *ICT and the Development of Techno-Pedagogical Skills among the Algerian University Teachers.* Journal of Educational and Social Research. Vl. 5. No. 1.

3. M, Leema & Saleem, M. (2017). *Infusion of Techno Pedagogy in Elementary Teacher Education Curriculum: Perspectives And Challenges.* IOSR Journal of Humanities and Social Science. Vol. 22. Issue. 2. pp. 6-10.

4. Prakas, J. & Hooda, S. (2017). *A Study of Techno-pedagogical Competency among Teachers of Government and Private Schools of Haryana State.* International Journal of Current Advanced Research. Vol. 7.

5. Bala, P. (2018). *An Examination of Techno-Pedagogical Competence and Anxiety towards the Use of Instructional Aids in Teaching among Senior Secondary School Teachers.* Chetana. Vol. 3. pp. 95-114.

6. Sana, et. al. (2018). *Exploring Teacher's Techno-Pedagogical Competence to Achieve Process Oriented Skills of Learners: A Multimedia Context.* Inquisitive Teacher. Vol. V. Issue II. pp. 174-188.

7. Anand, S. (2019). *Techno-pedagogical Competency of Faculty Members: The Present Need of Higher education.* Journal of Current Science. Vol. 20. Issue. 1

8. Islam, M. (2020). *Infusion of Techno-Pedagogy during Covid-19: Teachers' Perspective.* International Journal of Creative Research Thoughts. Vol. 8. Issue. 11.

9. Nayar, A. & Akmar, S. (2020). *Technology Pedagogical Content Knowledge (TPCK) and Techno Pedagogy Integration Skill (TPIS) Among Pre-Service Science Teachers- Case Study of a University Based ICT Based Teacher Education Curriculum.* Journal of Education and Practice. Vol. 11. pp.

14-65.

10. Asad, et. al. (2021). *Techno- Pedagogical Skills for 21ˢᵗ Century Digital Classrooms: An Extensive Literature Review.* Hindawi Journal.

11. Baregama, S. & Arora, R. (2021). *A Review of Studies on Techno-Pedagogical and Content Competencies.* Elementary Education Online. Vol. 20. Issue. 5

12. Rao, S. & B.N. Jalajakshi (2021). *Techno-Pedagogic Skills: An Indispensible Skill for a 21ˢᵗ Century Classroom Teacher.* International Journal of Creative Research Thoughts. Vol. 9. Issue. 3. pp. 1264-1267.

13. Sharma, N. & Sharma, R. (2021). *Techno-pedagogical Skills of Teacher Trainees Belonging to Arts and Science Academic Streams.* Towards Excellence: An Indexed, Referred & Peer Reviewed Journal of Higher Education. Vol. 13. Issue. 2. pp. 907-916.

14. Thirunavukkarasu, M. (2021). *Techno Pedagogical Skills among B.Ed. Student Teachers.* International Journal of All Research Education and Scientific Methods. Vol. 9.issue. 4.

CHAPTER TEN

Impact of the COVID-19 Pandemic on Higher Education in India: An Analytical Study

Sk Amiruddin*, Dr. Shweta Smrita Soy**

*Research Scholar, Department of Education, The University of Burdwan, West Bengal.

**Assistant Professor, Department of Education, The University of Burdwan, West Bengal.

Abstract

The COVID-19 pandemic stunned the whole world. Its effects are seen in all areas of human life. It is noxious to human beings. Education is also affected by the COVID-19 pandemic, especially the social distance or physical distance policies, which are more harmful for primary education and also activity-based higher education. During the COVID period, some developed countries organised education by using various technologies and the high-speed internet. But developing and under-developed countries face various problems in implementing technology-based online education. Policymakers face lots of problems in continuing the education system. India is an overpopulated and developing country. That is why the Indian education system during the COVID-19 pandemic was seriously hampered. During the COVID period, the students' reading habits, interaction, learning aspects, and mentality were completely hampered. Even in the post-COVID situation, most of the students lost their interest in learning. In the COVID era, online education, webinars, and virtual instruction are widely used in the field of education. The COVID-19 pandemic transformed the physical education concept to virtual education worldwide. Globalization, ICT, and the world economy have also promoted online learning in the field of higher education. But there were various problems with implementing online learning, especially in rural areas where people are not very aware of it.

The present paper addresses various problems of higher education in India during the COVID situation and also the present scenario of higher education in India.

Key words- COVID-19, Higher Education, Online Learning, Rural Areas.

Introduction

The COVID-19 pandemic forced the government or educational institutions to close their doors physically. Almost every government declared a lockdown and advised people to maintain a social distance to overcome the COVID-19 pandemic. All the educational institutions remained closed for a long time. During a long-term lockdown, higher education institutions implement e-learning to keep the education system running. Even primary schools have started an online teaching-learning process. The government of India initiated PM e-VIDYA, DIKSHA (one nation, one digital platform), MANODARPAN (for psychological support for the students), Swayam Prabha TV channel (for primary and secondary education), etc. for the betterment of the education system. During the COVID period, the Indian government spent a total of Rs. 5784.05 crores on education. This was done to fix the problem with the education system and keep it going.

During the COVID period, Indian higher educational institutions first adopted online approaches and used new technologies and infrastructure to continue the education system. Various private organisations give various suggestions and also prepare a lot of online learning apps, methods, techniques, etc. Students and teachers are becoming more comfortable with technology. A paradigm shift occurs in the field of education.

Objectives

The present paper focuses on the following objectives:

1. To examine the problem of higher education in India during the COVID-19 pandemic.

1. To find out the problems of higher education in India after the post COVID situation,

3. To understand the emerging trends with reference to higher Education.

4. To show the improvement of higher education in India.

Methodology

This paper is an analytical study. It is based on secondary data. The data has been collected from different government documents, different books, articles, and newspapers, five-year planning, national educational policy 2020, and reflective journals. Information is also collected from various articles and reports related to the COVID-19 pandemic, which were published by national and international agencies.

Higher Education in India During the COVID Situation

The Indian education sector was badly affected by the pandemic. All the educational institutions across the whole country were suddenly closed on March 16th 2020, when the central government announced the lockdown. Therefore, for a long time, all the educational institutions were completely closed across India. This long-term lockdown was harmful to the student's life. The students were demotivated and most of them were engaged in various online games, which were harmful for their learning. Students were mentally disturbed and missed the physical interaction with peers and teachers.

The COVID situation changes the pedagogy of the education system. Online learning, virtual education, webinars, and various technological concepts are widely used in the field of education. During the pandemic, primary education was completely closed for a long-time all-over India, but in the field of higher education, the government and educational institutions introduced new technologies for continuing education. During a COVID-situation, online learning is the main medium to continue education. Indian colleges and universities offer online classes, webinars, online quizzes, and other online activities to keep the education system going.

COVID-19 has numerous obstacles. The Indian government has responded constructively and implemented a variety of measures to deal with the pandemic's crisis. The Indian government has also adopted a variety of preventative measures to stop the epidemic from spreading. COVID-19. The MHRD and the University Grants Commission (UGC) have made several arrangements for students to continue their learning by launching a number of virtual platforms with online depositories, e-books and other online teaching-learning materials, educational channels via Direct to Home TV, and radios programme etc. Students use popular social media tools like WhatsApp, Zoom, Google Meet, Telegram, YouTube Live, Facebook Live, and others for online teaching and learning during lockdown.

Importance of Online Learning During Pandemic

Online education is continuing to grow rapidly with the help of technological innovations. During the past few decades, online education has spontaneously enlarged and its arrival has touched all sects of people, from old to young. Pupils can learn everything through the platforms of an online system. During the COVID-19 pandemic, the requirements of online education are enhanced. It is possible to learn better in a pandemic situation with the help of online platforms. Pupils can learn everything through the platforms of an online system. The following highlights the significance of the online instructional approach.

Learning from home: Through the process of online education, it is possible to learn better in a pandemic situation. With the help of an online platform, pupils can learn everything from home.

Time-management-Online learning approach is a very time-management system. If the time is utilised properly, then pupils can learn at any time based on their own situation. Many students spend a lot of time travelling because the distance from home to school is very long. But online education has greatly reduced the wastage of time.

Motivating the students: The online education system is very important for increasing the motivation of students. In this process, students learn and progress depends on the learner's self-motivation.

Continuation of education: Due to the lockdown, pupils must stay at home for their safety. But education is essential for the overall development of the personality. Online education provides such opportunities for teaching and learning while staying at home.

Virtual communication: The onlinesystem of education is helpful for virtual communication. With the help of technology, teachers and students can communicate with each other virtually.

Self-motivation: The students are eagerly participating in the online education system. This system helps to improve the technical skills of the pupils at school and college level. Actually, this system is important for self-motivated learning.

E-learning is emerging as the future trend of learning in India and will be dominant in the times ahead. E-learning has created new dimensions in education, both within and beyond the curriculum, and is still looking at further opportunities to become more practical. (Imran, 2012).

Barriers of Online Learning

Online education is quite a new concept in the field of education in India. That's why there are also some drawbacks to the online education system. In a study, Gaur et al. (2020) found that out of 394 participants, 241 (about 61%) agreed that they faced various obstacles during online classes. This approach to education is not as effective as a real classroom situation. Some barriers to the online instructional approach are:

Availability of e-learning materials: The success of e-learning mostly depends on the quality of learning materials. It is too difficult to prepare proper learning materials for all the children.

Lack of community involvement: Education is a social process and it occurs for the betterment of human beings. Education can't be excluded from society. But online learning is somewhat isolated from community involvement. (Pappas, 2006).

Lack of access to technology: Lack of technological knowledge is another barrier to the online education approach. Most of the pupils, about 40%, are facing technological problems. They are mainly in rural areas where the pupils are suffering the most. (Shahmoradi et al., 2018).

Language barrier: India is a very large and diverse country. It has thousands of local and vernacular languages. But most of the online course materials are written in English, and the medium of learning is also English. Therefore, students are facing a language problem, and they are not able to frequently communicate in the teaching-learning process.

Direct communication: As it is an online system, it is not possible to conduct face-to-face communication. Therefore, proper rapport and direct interaction between teacher and student are not possible.

Students' perception: The students faced various difficulties during online classes. Based on their own experiences, students' perceptions regarding online learning are negative. (Carr, 2000).

Network issues: Network issues are another disturbing factor for the online system of education. A poor network is a significant barrier to the online education system. Internet speed and signal strength are not equal all over India. There are various rural and remote areas which are still out of 4G coverage areas. Even, there are some areas in India where electricity is not yet properly available.

Lack of awareness: India is a populated country. But most of the people are not aware of online learning, and people give least importance to online learning.

Lack of social interaction: Inonline learning, student-teacher communication, student-to-student communication or social communication is somehow hampered. Therefore, students feel a lack of social interaction.

Addiction to online games: Most of the time, students are addicted to online games and social networking sites and they neglect their studies. Actively and frequently participating in social networking sites and online games can negatively affect their grades or hamper their progress towards their future careers.

Students' activeness: The students have how much interest in this process of learning and if they only join their class without their interest, it's not possible to determine. Therefore, the quality of the teaching-learning process is questionable.

Not cost-effective: The cost of online learning is quite high. In India, where the majority of people are busy to collect food for two days, they would not be able to spend money on purchasing some basic substances (e.g., smartphones, laptops, the internet, and so on) that are required for online learning.

Lack of motivation: students' low motivation is another problem of online learning. Some students feel boredom in the online class. (Maltby & Whittle, 2000).

Therefore, various debates and discussions are going on about the quality of online education and the future of students. In a developing country such as India, the number of students and educational institutions or boards is increasing rapidly, but the quality of online education is still a big question. Therefore, to the learner, online education should be low-cost, flexible, quality-based, and facile. Also, students' motivation, perception, engagement, and preference are important factors for online learning.

Problems of Higher Education in India after the Post-COVID Situation

One by one, more powerful variants of COVID arise and affect the people. That is why parents, teachers and students have different views on whether schools or colleges should reopen. Most of them wanted to re-open the schools and colleges and continue face-to-face education following the COVID-19 protocol advised by WHO (World Health Organization), the central government and different educational institutions across the country. After school reopened, students are having trouble getting motivated, having health problems, getting headaches, and other problems. Besides that, there is a lack of teaching aids, sanitization of the building, low attendance of students, national and international students' mobility were reduced, etc. The COVID situation seriously hampered the educational assessment system. Most of the external examinations were either cancelled or postponed. Even in a post-COVID situation, students pressurise educational institutions to conduct the online examination. They did not agree to give an offline examination. This means that most students are not prepared for the examinations. Students feel anxiety and uncertainty about their ability. This has a direct effect on students' future lives and also national development.

Emerging Trends in Higher Education in India

Education has emerged as the top priority for nations globally. Higher education's purpose is not limited to encouraging the economic development of nations and providing individuals with opportunities; it also includes the promotion of cultural variety, political democracy, national development, and international trade. India also has a rich heritage culture. To promote, preserve, and transform it for a new generation, education is essential. Higher education can assist society and international cooperation more effectively. In the 19th and 20th centuries, higher education was altered to fit the needs of the rising national industrial sector. Higher education is changing again, this time to meet the needs of a digital information economy that works around the world.

The Indian higher education system is the third largest in the world. The Indian higher education system faces a number of obstacles but has ample chances to overcome these obstacles and significantly improve the system. Since independence, the number of universities and colleges in India's higher education sector has increased dramatically. Before the new Indian education policy of 2020, higher education began after the intermediate level (i.e., ten years of primary and secondary education and two years of senior secondary education). The New Education Policy 2020 is the first education policy of the 21st century and replaces the National Policy on Education, which has existed for thirty-four years. The reform of the higher education system into tiers one, two, and three by the New Education Policy 2020 This restructure could facilitate the dissemination of research culture at the undergraduate level. Tier one consists of research universities that focus equally on research and teaching. Tier two consists of teaching universities that focus largely on teaching, and Tier three consists of undergraduate-only teaching colleges. The "Right to Education Act," which mandates compulsory and free education for all children aged six to fourteen, has brought about a change in the country's educational system. Higher educational institutions, such as colleges and universities, are currently delivering youth empowerment through quality-based training and research education. Emerging new trends such as artificial intelligence, individualised learning, wellness initiatives, and teacher learning programmes, etc. India faces obstacles in higher education. As a result, a greater number of new trends are emerging at a faster rate to enhance students' abilities and broaden their worldview. The game changers for Indian higher education are globalization, the COVID-19 pandemic, the advancement of ICT and the attitude of the government towards education. Indian higher education is now used to virtual learning, open and distance learning, and e-learning.

Some Remedies for the Betterment of Higher Education

In the present situation, our world has been facing some critical challenges. Approximately two years ago, our world faced the detrimental COVID-19, which stopped the development of human civilization. In the pandemic, various critical problems are arising in the world, such as unemployment, economic loss, underdevelopment, slow growth, health issues, loss in the field of education, etc. At present, with the help of technological innovation, man can control the loss of education. Educators and learners should be trained in how to use technology to facilitate online teaching and learning. Students also need to be supported with improved internet connectivity and technology, which most students cannot afford. Therefore, governments and educational institutions should adopt policies to provide free internet access and digital devices to all students in order to encourage online learning, which would keep people engaged. The government should provide more assistance to higher education institutions. Educational institutions should concentrate on virtual educational activities, such as education via television, radio, and the internet, etc. Besides that, educational institutions must promote knowledge sharing and peer learning for restorative educational losses and organise seminars, symposiums, and debates to make up for lost learning.

Conclusion

The COVID-19 pandemic disrupted the lives of all spare human beings. It has harmfully affected all fields of mankind. To overcome the spread of COVID-19 effects, educational institutions were completely shut down, but later, considering the futures of students, online learning was adopted to continue the teaching-learning process. The COVID situation changed the pedagogy of education from physical learning to e-learning. E-learning provides learners the opportunity to continue their studies. But e-learning is a new concept for the learner, and that's why there are various problems. Policymakers and educational institutions are trying to resolve those problems. During the COVID period, the central government published NEP-2020, which also focused on the quality of higher education and technology-based education. To ensure quality, NEP 2020 gave importance to holistic and multidisciplinary education, vocationalization of higher education, effective governance and leadership development, inclusiveness of higher education etc. In the new normal, students and teachers could use e-learning and other technology-based ways to teach and learn, as well as private apps and teaching methods that were made during the COVID-19 period.

References

Bozkurt, A., & Sharma, R. C. (2020). Education in normal, new normal and next normal: Observations from the past, insights from the present and projections for the future. *Asian Journal of Distance Education*, 15(2), Retrieved from https://doi.org/10.5281/zenodo.4362664

Jena, P. K. (2020). Impact of pandemic covid -19 on education in India. *International Journal of Current Research*. 12(07), 12582-12586

Kapasia, N., Paula, P., Roy, A., Saha, J., Zaveri, A., Mallick, R., Barman, B., Das, P. & Chouhan, P. (2020). Impact of lockdown on learning status of undergraduate and postgraduate students during Covid-19 pandemic in West Bengal, India. *Children and Youth Services Review*. *116*(105194), Retrieved from https://doi.org/10.1016/j.childyouth.2020.105194

Morales, V. J., Moreno, A.G. & Rojas, R. M. (2021). The Transformation of Higher Education After the Covid Disruption: Emerging Challenges in an Online Learning Scenario. *Forntiers in Psychology*. Retrieved from https://doi.org/10.3389/fpsyg.2021.616059

Rashid, S. & Yadav, S.S. (2020). Impact of Covid-19 Pandemic on Higher Education and Research. *Indian Journal of Human Development*. DOI: 10.1177/0973703020946700

Saha, T., Das, P.P. & Singh, R. (2021). Challenges in higher education during and after Covid-19 pandemic in India. *Journal of Physics: Conference Series*. 1797 (2021) 012065 IOP Publishing doi:10.1088/1742-6596/1797/1/012065

Song, L. & Hill, R. (2007). A Conceptual Model for Understanding Self-Directed Learning in Online Environments. *Journal of Interactive Online*

Learning www.ncolr.org/jiol Volume 6, Number 1, ISSN: 1541-4914.

Tarkar, P. (2020). Impact of Covid-19 Pandemic on Education System. *International Journal of Advanced Science and Technology* Vol. 29, No. 9s, pp. 3812-3814 ISSN: 2005-4238 IJAST

Teras, M., Suoranta, J., Teras, H. & Curcer, M. (2020). Post-Covid-19 Education and Education Technology 'Solutionism': a Seller's Market. *Postdigital Science and Education.* 2, 863–878, Retrieved from https://doi.org/10.1007/s42438-020-00164-x

COVID-19 AND STUDENTS' MENTAL WELL-BEING: A LONG PROCESS OF STRUGGLES AND HEALING

Rakesh Bag[1], Dr. Kalyani Mitra[2]

Research Scholar, Department of Education, JIS University, Agarpara, West Bengal, India[1]

Assistant Professor, Department of Education, JIS University, Agarpara, West Bengal, India[2]

Kalyani.mitra@jisuniversity.ac.in, rakeshbag01@gmail.com

ABSTRACT

A healthy classroom environment is meant to reduce anxiety, increase attention and help emotional and behavioral changes in a student. While such an environment is desired for every student at every level of their study, the COVID-19 pandemic has changed that scenario and has left deep emotional wounds in the minds of both students and teachers. The spread of COVID-19 has disrupted every aspect of human life. In order to maintain the mandates of physical distancing the face-to-face(offline) teaching and learning process stopped, resulting in the schools remaining closed for a long time. Missing out face to face interactions and spend quality time with their friends and staying cooped in the home while fearing the day-to-day uncertainty have taken a great toll on the mental state of students. There was a substantial spike in the deterioration of mental well-being among students during the pandemic situation when the school close for a long time and they could not go to school. Online classes could not fulfill the emotional as well as mental needs of young, impressionable minds. Severely worsened mental health often led to acute anxiety, stress, panic attacks and depression. Sometimes, it even affected the mental well-being of a student. But due to the prejudices and taboos that have remained stuck to the idea of getting curative measures for mental health in our country, lots of students could not able to, or could not even considered asking for professional help during this time. This article highlights on the effects of Covid-19 on students Mental Health.

Keywords: COVID 19, Mental Well-being, Anxiety, Depression, Stress,

INTRODUCTION

Mental health includes our behavioral, social, psychological, and emotional well-being. When a person feels, think and behave normally and also absence of mental disorder it indicates that the persons is in a good mental state. When Quarantine happens a sick person or a person who is at the risk of getting sick of some infectious disease is isolated from other people in a safe environment for a specific amount of time. When the person is deemed by a medical professional to be safe from getting sick or spreading the contagion to other people the quarantine ends and the person is allowed to come out of his/her isolated state of living. Since the pandemic caused the authorities to close the schools for an uncertain amount of time, the mental well-being of the students had become especially vulnerable during this.

Asking for professional help for psychiatric reasons has been frowned upon and considered to be a taboo in the society. Going for therapy make you sick in the eyes of the society and this ailment is considered much more dangerous compared to cancer. However, mental health is as grave a cause of concern as physical health. Both aspects need to be taken care of in order to achieve a healthy state of being. People can recover from their mental disorders with the help of right expertise of a professional and the society needs to shake off the stigmas which associated with seeking help and therapy. The issue of mental health is being enunciated all over the world. Awareness camp arranged for the students and their parents to know the effect of COVID-19 on their mental health and daily lives. Because that is the only way to become resilient enough to cope with the emotional trauma inflicted by a pandemic and its aftermath.

CONCEPTUAL FRAMEWORK

MENTAL HEALTH

Mental health is very much needed to lead a quality life. It is a condition when average person feel good mentally and physically. The term "Mental Health" includes our psychological, emotional and social well-being. Mental health is an essential and integral part of health mere absence of illness, of an individual's daily life. Mental health regulates what an individual thinks about other person and the ability to face the realities of daily life.

Sound mental health is required for a person to balance his/her emotional responses, desires, creativity and competence output.

COVID-19 PANDEMIC

This infectious pandemic disease was first identified in the month of December 2019 in Wuhan, China. On 30 January 2020 WHO declared the outbreak a public Health Emergency of International Concern and a pandemic on 11 March, 2020.The COVID 19 Pandemic is caused by the virus known as Corona virus 2 (SARS-CoV-2). COVID 19 created an ongoing pandemic situation caused by several acute respiratory syndrome. Mainly this disease spreads very first when peoples are in close proximity. It spreads very easily and sustainably, primarily via contaminated droplets produced during breathing, coughing sneezing, talking and singing. Especially in indoor spaces some can be suspended in air as aerosols though many larger droplets rapidly fall to the ground. It can also spread from completely asymptomatic people that's why testing is an important measure in the prevention of COVID-19. The infection can persist for 7-12 days in moderate cases, and up to two weeks in severe cases.

OBJECTIVES

The present study is focused on the following objectives

- To find out the effect of COVID 19 on student's mental health.
- To highlight the Challenges faced by students on virtual platform.
- To analyze the Importance of school and classroom environment.
- To highlight the probable causes of suicidal tendency in students in this pandemic situation.
- To know the cause of facing anxiety or stress during lockdown.
- To highlight the changes in sleeping pattern of the students in this pandemic situation.
- To analyze the problem faced by the student regarding concentration in study time and also in any other work in his daily life.

RESEARCH METHODOLOGY

This study is based on the basis of various data collected from authentic websites, journals, articles, e-contents, from internet relating to COVID 19 and struggles of student's mental health. The date has been taken from various reports of National and International Agencies to carry out the present study.

MAJOR FINDINGS/RESULT AND DISCUSSION

CHALLENGES FACED BY STUDENTS ON VIRTUAL PLATFORM

One of the measures that have been actively being practiced to stave off the resurgence of the pandemic is maintaining a physical distance through 'social distancing'. During the pandemic, having classes while remaining indoors or at home had become the only viable alternative to school. But being idle in home had become one of the major factors of rapidly growing mental stress for the students. Online teaching has taken up the mantle of keeping the learning process from getting completely stagnant. While this system had its own problems, online learning was very useful solution in this situation. Stakeholders of school have tried to adapt the teaching-learning process with this new, changing and challenging circumstance. The interactions between the students and teacher have also undergone changes due to the changes in the medium of teaching.

IMPORTANCE OF SCHOOL AND CLASSROOM ENVIRONMENT

The teacher has a crucial role in keeping the students attentive and their minds active in their studies using different attractive teaching learning tools and a well-thought-out lesson plan. Learning through teamwork on different projects helps the students to hone their collaborative, cooperative and leadership skills. It also aids them in choosing their areas of interest which would further help in their learning. Improvement in language skills, reading skills, listening skills, and comprehension skills also become important in this regard. The mother-language, arts, social science and sciences are topics that are significant in releasing the creativity and the appreciation for the world in general and own culture in particular in a child. A wholesome learning approach encourages the children to grow up while learning how to share things with other children and enjoying things together. For this reason, keeping a positive, healthy and friendly teaching learning environment in school is highly desired.

SUICIDAL TENDENCY IN STUDENTS

The social behavior and the social exposure of children have been negatively impacted by the closing of schools and the advent of online classes. During the pandemic situation when school closed for a long-time student have been deprived from the healthy classroom which provides a social circle for the students and decrease stress and anxiety. The development of suicidal tendency in students can be attributed to social isolation, anxiety, fear of contagion, uncertainty, chronic stress and economic difficulties. The students who had lost their family members or friends to COVID-19 have also gone through a traumatic experience during the pandemic. Students who were already patients of mental disorders had to experience an upsurge during this time. Students can be split into two categories based on whether they have professional help for their conditions or not. The feeling of helplessness and anguish have given rise to stress, anxiety, fear, anger, depression and in the most extreme cases suicidal behaviors. Suicide in general, and suicide among young people in particular have been considered a grave health problem that is also related to mental health Many countries across the world are struggling to address and mitigate this issue.

PROBLEM IN CONCENTRATION

The lock-down and prolonged online classes due to the schools being closed to ensure the safety of the students forced students of all classes and academic levels to resort to distant learning. But it has been seen that online classes do not hold the attention of students like an offline class where the students, teacher and the teaching tools are tangibly present in close quarters. The online class creates a mental distance which makes it easy for the concentration needed to grasp an educational subject to vccr off its course. Several other factors like the constant nervousness about the COVID-19 situation throughout the world affected the mental health which in turn adversely affected the attention span among the students. Panic disorder, anxiety, and depression also led to an increase of unhappiness and decrease of attention span for studies. While positive emotions are a good way to energies the mind and encourage it to undertake new ventures and scopes of studies, whereas negative emotions work just opposite effect.

CHANGE IN SLEEPING PATTERN

Having a healthy sleeping pattern is one of the major factors of being healthy. Students can be often seen suffering with their sleep schedules because of too much study-load, and worries regarding adolescence and the onset of early adulthood. The COVID-19 inevitably was a cause for worsening sleep situation among the students all over the world. Disturbed sleep and increase in the frequency of nightmares resulted from the lockdowns and tensions over the fluctuating graph of COVID-19 all over the world. A bad sleeping pattern is bound to negatively affect the physical and mental well-being of a student. Unhealthy food and irregular consumption due to stress and a financially unstable situation in many cases led to bad health as well. Several works have shown that nightmares and increased cases of sleep- paralysis have been a cause for concern among students as has been the rise of anxiety. This gave birth to a harmful cycle of irritability, less concentration and further sluggishness due to the lack of sleep among young and young adult students, whether they are in middle of their careers or they are trying to choose their career path.

FACING ANXIETY OR STRESS DURING LOCK DOWN

Anxiety disorder is something that many people experience these days. Panic disorder or long bouts of depression that can sometimes last a lifetime are also potential results of this. Students of different age-groups, academic levels and family and economical backgrounds had to struggle with anxiety during the peak of the pandemic, as well as after the pandemic abated to a certain degree and an extent of normalcy could be achieved. Since the students experience different circumstances and every individual is their own person, the cause of anxiety can also vary from individual to individual. For example, an elementary school student might be facing serious issues about the sudden lack of outdoor activities and decreased social interaction during a foundational time when friendships just start budding. At the same time, a high school student might be anxious about his/her future career and interpersonal relationships with his/her peers and teachers. Anxiety disorder can cure with time; it cannot project a hasty development even if the object or situation that was causing the disorder gets removed or erased from the sufferer's life. Due to this reason, when the spreading of COVID-19 has receded for a while in many countries and schools have gone back to holding almost regular offline classes and activities, many students are yet to come out of the clutch the mental disorders that they have been experiencing. The need for personal effort and support from surrounding people is very useful for recovering from anxiety. With that I think that repairing the mental damage caused by the pandemic on the students' mental health will not be a quick or easy process.

CONCLUSION

Throughout the world, students' insecurities and worries about their studies, career and future when the pandemic was reaching its peak in different countries and had seen an exponential growth. Students who already had an existing mental health condition since before the pandemic were greatly vulnerable during this time as the fear of going outside the house had a detrimental effect on the issue of continuing their treatment or therapy. As can be seen in this discussion, number of schools drop-outs increased, as did the suicidal tendencies in students.

Even after the pandemic has waned(indefinitely) in many countries across the globe, students who were cooped up in their homes or residences for the past two years are finding it difficult to go back to school and the keep up with the active classroom environment. In this scenario it is up to the teachers and the parents to take up the mantle of support and make sure that the changing atmosphere is something that the students can handle this situation with strong mentality. Taking time to listen to the concerns of the students, welcoming their feedback on both teaching and the teaching environment and promoting sports and social interactions among students are some of the ways in which teachers and parents can try to ensure that shifts in their surroundings does not overwhelm the mental well-being of the students. Sound physical health and mental well-being are needed to properly pursue the studies and helping the students find improve their footholds once again is the most important task right now.

REFERENCES

Edginton, A., Holbrook, J. (2010). *A Blended Learning Approach to Teaching Basic Pharmacokinetics and the Significance of Face-to-Face Interaction.* Retrieved on January 10, 2022 from, https://www.semanticscholar.org/paper/A-Blended-Learning-Approach-to-Teaching-Basic-and-Edginton-Holbrook/ e0c27018cdb3d08d337616d8edbb7c2ef15cc2a7

Ali, J. K. M. (2017). *Blackboard as a Motivator for Saudi EFL Students: A Psycholinguistic Study.* Retrieved on March 15, 2022 from, https://pdfs.semanticscholar.org/d584/ 1093e63c8c36df6b16361da030fb90acd0b6.pdf.

Kayyali, M. (2020). *Post COVID-19: New Era for Higher Education Systems.* Retrieved on March 11, 2022 from, https://www.researchgate.net/publication/ 347923984_Post_COVID-19_New_Era_for_Higher_Education_Systems

Marinoni, G., Van't Land, H., & Jensen, T. (2020). *The impact of Covid-19 on higher education around the world.* IAU Global Survey Report. Retrieved on January 12, 2022 from, https://www.iau-aiu.net/IAU-Global-Survey-on-the-Impact-of-COVID-19-on-Higher-Education-around-the

Mohammad, M. (2020). *Challenges of e-Learning during the COVID-19 Pandemic Experienced by EFL Learners.* Retrieved on January 22, 2022 from, https://files.eric.ed.gov/fulltext/EJ1287713.pdf

Simpson, J. C. (2020). Distance learning during the early stages of the COVID-19 pandemic: Examining K-12 students' and parents' experiences and perspectives. Retrieved on January 15, 2022 from, http://www.mifav.uniroma2.it/inevent/events/idea2010/doc/46_2.pdf

Bansal, R. (2021). *Higher Education Sector in India: Disruptions By COVID-19 And Post Covid Trends.* Retrieved on February 14, 2022 from,

Huck, C., Zhang J. (2021). *Effects of the COVID-19 Pandemic on K-12 Education: A Systematic Literature Review.* Retrieved on February 18, 2022 from, https://files.eric.ed.gov/fulltext/EJ1308731.pdf

PROSPECTS AND CHALLENGES OF BLENDED LEARNING IN THE PRESENT EDUCATIONAL SCENARIO

Anjum Sahidullah

Research Scholar (PhD), Department of Education, Cotton University, Guwahati, Assam

Abstract:

Education is one of the areas which have experienced significant challenges due to the outbreak of the Corona virus, COVID -19. This pandemic lead to the closure of schools, colleges and universities worldwide. India too was no exception. Considering the educational scenario in India, the University Grants Commission and other apex bodies of education decided to undertake education through online modes. Education system in India also came up with various new opportunities along with several challenges. Nowadays the trend of e-learning is increasing and one of the tools to implement this concept is through Blended Learning. Blended learning is a mixture of learning methods which includes multiple teaching modals- most frequently e-learning and traditional face-to-face learning. The objective of any successful blended learning program is to differentiate instruction to meet the learning needs of all students. The quality of blended learning approach lies in the adaptation of technology aided learning methods in addition to the existing traditional based learning. Blended learning is an approach to education which combines online educational materials and opportunities for interaction online with traditional place-based classroom methods. The paper attempts to study the prospects of blended learning in the present education scenario. It also highlights some of the challenges faced by blended learning.

Keywords: Blended learning, Challenges, Prospects, Traditional Learning

Introduction:

Education is one of the areas which have experienced significant challenges due to the outbreak of the Corona virus, COVID -19. This pandemic lead to the closure of schools, colleges and universities worldwide. India too was no exception. Considering the educational scenario in India, the University Grants Commission and other apex bodies of education decided to undertake education through online modes. Although SWAYAM, EDUSAT, National Digital Repository, INFLIBNET, etc are some of the efforts which have been taken by the Indian government to provide and support e-learning, much needs to be done in this direction. Education system in India also has come up with various new opportunities along with several challenges Nowadays the trend of e-learning is increasing and one of the tools to implement this concept is through Blended Learning. Blended learning is fast becoming a preferred teaching strategy for all grade levels. It is a potential outcome of advanced technology based learning system. Blended learning is a mixture of learning methods which incorporates multiple teaching modals- most frequently e-learning and traditional face-to-face learning. So, Blended learning is considered as a proper mix of various media to maximize learning experience with minimum utility of resources to ensure optimum realization of educational objectives, by making the perfect blend of information technology and instructional technology. In this era of globalization and digitalization, technologies are becoming an integral part of day to day life and in near future blended learning will be synonymous with learning.

Blended learning offers flexible time frames which can be personalized to each person, offering them the ability to learn at their own pace. The objective of any successful blended learning program is to differentiate instruction to meet the learning needs of all students. The quality of blended learning approach lies in the adaptation of technology aided learning methods in addition to the existing traditional based learning. Blended learning is an approach to education which combines online educational materials and opportunities for interaction online with traditional place-based classroom methods. Infact, Blended learning incorporates direct instruction, indirect instruction, collaborative teaching, individualized computer assisted learning.

Characteristics of Blended Learning

Blended learning is a mix of classic and modern learning method. Some characteristics of blended learning involve the following:

a. Face to face teaching- Blended learning provides full scope for traditional classroom teaching where students get ample time to interact with their teachers and thus get influenced by their personality, behaviour and value system.
b. Support for learners- Another characteristic that blended learning programs share is the support available for learners. Trainers working in these programs offer learners all the support they need both through offline meetings and online solution.
c. Webinars- Webinar is another characteristic of blended learning that is ICT supported format. Students participate in seminars in different topics appropriate to them via internet connection.
d. Viewing expert lectures in YouTube- Blended learning provides student to take advantage of the experts of the course content they are studying as they can easily watch the different lectures by renowncd experts from different fields available on YouTube's. In addition to it college can upload video of lecture by its own teacher so that if student is not able to attend the college he can avail this facility and can gain benefit of the teachers teaching.

Difference between Blended Learning and Traditional Learning

There are certain differences between Blended learning and Traditional Learning which may be enumerated below:

1. **Effective Learning:** Blended learning is more effective than traditional methods because learners can focus on content while using their self-paced online material on their own time.
2. **Customized Content:** In a traditional classroom setting, learners are of many. The individual needs of learners are not taken into consideration and they are merged into a "one-size-fits-all" curriculum. Learners only work on what is relevant and important specific to them with blended learning program.
3. **No Fear Factor:** With blended learning program, anxiety over tests and grades or fear of failing are eliminated since the pass/fail of a traditional learning environment is irrelevant.

4. **Flexibility:** Blended learning allows for instant access to information anywhere in the world, as long as the learner has a computer or a Smartphone and an internet connection. Live instruction whether face-to-face or virtual is built around the learner's availability and provides greater flexibility, unlike the traditional learning environments where learners have to attend classes at a fixed date and time.

Different Levels of Blended Learning:

1. **Activity-level blending:** Activity-level blending occurs "when a learning activity contains both face-to-face and computer mediated elements". Today's smart classroom falls under this category.
2. **Course level blending:** Courselevel blending is a "combination of distinct face-to-face and computer mediated activities used as part of a course".
3. **Program-level blending:** Program-level blending occurs when participants choose a mix between courses that have to be face-to-face courses and online courses or in which the combination between the two is prescribed by the program.
4. **Institutional level blending:** Institutional level blending occurs when there is a institutional level commitment to blending face to face and computer mediated instruction and in which they create or endorse models at an institutional level.

Prospects of Blended Learning:

Blended learning includes various teaching methods to enhance the cognitive abilities of the students and to make the education system much efficient and effective. Some of the prospects of blended learning in the present education system can be highlighted with the following points:

1. **Boosts learners' efficiency:** With blended learning, learning managers can provide learners with instant access to their learning materials wherever they need them. This is because blended learning relies partly on technology and all the learning materials are accessible online. Due to that ease of access, learners can learn at their own pace and acquire the necessary knowledge and skills in the way which best fits their individual learning styles.

2. **Builds engagement:** One of the biggest difficulties for learning managers is engaging the students and keeping them interested in the learning materials. In such a situation, effective blended learning is the best way forward. Blended learning helps learners to engage themselves in continuous process of learning at their own pace.

3. **Improves collaboration:** Collaboration is one of the key factors necessary for effective learning. Blended learning enables the course participants to work together, engage in discussion and provide useful feedback to one another which undoubtedly leads to improvement and higher engagement.

4. **Keeping track of learners' progress:** Blended learning enables the teacher to keep track of learners' progress at any given time so that the teacher can understand their strengths and weaknesses.

5. **Ensures effective mix of learning methods:** Blended learning represents a formal education program which brings together the best of classroom and online learning. Learners and educators like blended learning because it complements the classroom learning in the right way.

6. **Affordability:** Blended learning techniques are much affordable for the students as well as for the teachers. The students who are involved in some part time job can assess the tutorials in their time of ease and in the case of teachers they can deliver the online lectures anywhere at any time.

7. **Self regulatory learning:** Blended learning offers the advantages of self regulatory learning and ease of revision for the self motivated learners.

8. **Improves student'sacademic performance:** According to different research studies, blended learning is effective in both teaching and learning which improves the student's academic performance.

Challenges of Blended Learning:

Inspite of having many prospects, Blended Learning also faces some challenges. These challenges have been discussed below:

1. The first thing which comes to mind when we think of the disadvantages of blended learning is the cognitive load. New to the blended model, some teachers may start over delivering content and educational activities.

2. Acquiring software technology and hardware for blended learning program may sometimes become costly.

3. One of the key issues is the technological literacy which can be a real problem for teachers.

4. There is negative attitude towards new technology among some of the teachers. The teachers do not want to adapt to new methodologies and ways of teaching-learning.

5. Blended learning makes teachers overwork. Teachers involved in all stages of blended learning also face a great deal of additional work. They have to broaden their horizons, choose the most suitable syllabus and apply significantly more of their time and effort to discover the right balance between online and face-to-face learning. Unfortunately, all of them are not willing to do so.

6. The challenge for implementation of blended learning in higher institutions is time commitment. Developing a blended learning course usually takes two to three times the amount of time required to develop a similar course in a traditional format.

7. Technical support for course design may be lacking. This results from insufficient interrelation between the information and communication technology (ICT) experts and faculty members offering blended learning courses.

Conclusion:

No reform in education is likely to succeed without the active participation and ownership of teachers. Successful pedagogical use of technology depends on teacher's attitude and acceptance towards technology. It should be taken into that the successful use of e-learning platforms depends on the teachers having knowledge about the use of materials and imparting the knowledge to the learners in its use in proper context. Learners can be benefitted to a great extent by using the e-learning materials through blended learning process. Blended learning is not only useful for learners in the process of learning but it is also helpful for teacher training process, school education system, leadership training and many more. Moreover, Blended learning benefits students, teachers, administrators and even a layman who wants to acquire knowledge in any field of learning and of interest. Thus, it is hoped that blended learning if implemented properly can play a significant role in Indian education in posterity.

References

Das, D. A. (2016). E-Learning Paradigm: Virtual Learning, Mobile Learning and Blended Learning. In D. P. Das, *Contemporary Issues of Indian Education* (pp. 16-43). Guwahati: Shanti Prakashan.

Jayanthi, R. (2019). A Study about Blended Learning- Its Importance and Concept. *International Journal of Scientific Development and Research (IJSDR)*, 387-397.

Kalita, I. (2019). Blended Learning:A Paradigm Shift in the Process of Teaching-Learning. In D. U. Sarma, *Recent Trends in Education* (pp. 194-201). Delhi: Akhand Publishing House.

Kaur, M. (2013). Blended Learning-Its Challenges and future. *Procedia*, 612-617.

Khan, A. I., Qayyum, N. u., Shaik, M. S., Ali, A. M., & Bebi, C. V. (2012). Study of Blended Learning Process in Education Context. *International Journal of Modern Education and Computer Science*.

CHAPTER THIRTEEN

Education: From disruption to recovery

Sajda Khatun M.A (Education), B.Ed.

Abstract

With the sudden outbreak of Covid-19, the lives of people have changed worldwide. The education system was the most affected sector. The complete lockdown prevented students- teachers from attending school physically. Without any research and analysis, the adaptation of the digital teaching-learning process led to the disruption of the education system. With lot of trial and error, the experimental implementation helped to survive the system. In this post-pandemic, educational institutions are reforming themselves to cover up the losses. In this context, the researcher took the help of the secondary data available online to analyse the present scenario of the educational institutions; how performance and assessment tests were taken during a pandemic, and how it is reforming after two years. The researcher collected data on -what efforts were taken by the Government, NGOs, school management, and higher education authorities to maintain the quality of education and how they are moulding themselves with the need of the time. The challenges of the teachers are studied for further research to improve the mental health of the students and the entire education system in post-pandemic period. On basis of that some measures can be taken to improve the overall system in a systematic way.

Keywords

Traditional Classroom, Digital learning, mental health, online teaching-learning

Introduction

The upheaval caused due to the storm of COVID-19 affected the entire education system vulnerably. At the very beginning, the consequences were unpredictable. Health and survival of lives were the first priority of every individual. The decision to close educational institutions for an uncertain period was appreciated globally. Students' happiness had no limit; parents with mixed emotions did not know how to react as the pandemic threw normal life out of gear. People around the world held the pause button of life hoping everything will get normalized soon.

After spending a few months inside the four walls, the caged life became exhausted and a rapid return to normal life was on everyone's lips. As per the need of the time, people started moving out for their livelihood but no one dared to risk their children's lives by sending them to educational institutions. As a result, online teaching-learning was embraced globally but with the sudden announcement of the digitalization of the education system theoretically changed the mode but implementation needed a lot of trial and error which led to the disruption. There was no one size fit for everyone. Adaptation is a part of survival; by keeping that view in mind, students- teachers- parents' collaborative contributions reshaped the education system.

Various Digital tools were not available for everyone, in some places availability of an internet connection was a major hindrance, different age groups needed various pedagogical content, and assessment and evaluation required training and technical support. The experimental process gave rise to an advanced method of teaching where the blended method, the Hybrid model of teaching became the regular vocabulary that was added to the dictionary of the students and teachers. The waves came to push us into the new one to find the shore. The disrupted system is still recovering in its new attire.

The incorporated technology in the education system has been embraced by everyone around the world which may have a brighter side; that will reflect with time. The pandemic has disrupted education system but has not destructed. Rather disruption is the beginning of new formation.

Literature Review

- Pratap, H & Singh, R (2021) worked on "Review on the New Education System after COVID-19". The article highlighted the emerging opportunity and challenges of the new education system. In addition to curriculum studies, this article suggests that other options for education should be discussed in order to consider education with the current COVID-19 pandemic.

- Dar, S. Ahmad & Lone, N.Ahmad (2021) worked on " Impact of Covid-19 on Education in India". This Research paper put some light on the growth of EdTech start-ups during times of pandemics and natural disasters and includes suggestions for academic institutions on how to deal with challenges associated with online learning.

- Bansal, R & Pruthi, N (2021) worked on "HIGHER EDUCATION SECTOR IN INDIA: DISRUPTIONS BY COVID-19 AND POST COVID TRENDS". This article aims at assessing the disruption of COVID-19 as well as post covid trend in the Indian higher education sector. The finding of this study shows that this disruption may have an everlasting impact on this sector and it is concluded that it is important to assess the post covid trend too.

- Babbar, M & Gupta, T elucidate in their article entitled "Response of educational institutions to COVID-19 pandemic: An inter-country comparison" the extraordinary challenges faced by various stakeholders in making the move to digital learning and the significant efforts to minimize learning losses made by educational institutions.

- **Tuba, T & Illiyan, A (2021) worked on "School teachers' perception and challenges towards online teaching during COVID-19 pandemic in India: an econometric analysis". This study is pertinent to examine teachers' perceptions of online teaching and the obstacles they face in online teaching during this pandemic. The study shows that teachers are confronted with many challenges in virtual classes.**

Objective of the study

This study will focus on

• Different strategies applied by educational institutions in the post-pandemic period to recover the disrupted education system in India

• To find out the difficulties faced by the educational institutions to go back into the previous traditional classroom teaching.

• The role of teachers, facilitators, researchers, educational experts, and Government from the time of disruption till the recovery phase to reshape the entire system.

Methodology

In this descriptive research, the available literature; related to the education system during COVID-19 and post COVID period in India have been used as a source of secondary data. The data are collected online through different Government and Non-Government websites, magazines,

Journals, articles, e-contents, newspapers and reports to study the current situation of the educational institutions and to analyze their problems.

Virus into the system: A Disruption

The dreadful impact of coronavirus is shown in every system. Immediately it affected the health system over the world. The education system was not spared from this deadly disease. The school closure due to COVID-19 has brought significant disruption to the education system across the world. According to UNESCO, 120 crore students' education got disrupted due to school closure. In India, this number is approx 32.1 crores. Keeping children at home for such a long period of time has disturbed the physical and emotional well-being of children. The academic gap has been shortened by digital education but the students of the disadvantaged groups were not privileged to access digital learning due to poverty and they are the most affected section of the education sector. For the overall development of the education system, many initiatives have been taken by the Government, schools, teachers, and NGOs for the recovery of the disrupted system. The following details will throw light on how the recovery is taking place from the disruption in the post-pandemic situation.

Classroom Environment- Educational institutions were compelled to adopt the digital mode of learning to bring the students' habit of learning. The transition from traditional classrooms to online classrooms without any planning has not been easy at all, at least in India, which has a major remote population. In 2014, a report by the Indian government Planning Commission estimated that 363 million Indians, making up 29.5% of the total population, were living below the poverty line in 2011-12. It was challenging for the entire education sector to digitize the education system. Poverty and lack of access to learning materials became the major roadblock of the e-classroom. To reduce the wide gap between rich and poor students, the central government has introduced the PM e-VIDYA platform, a platform with 12 new DTH channels; one for each class, that will cater to the needs of everyone in society. In spite of various efforts taken by the Government, every student did not get the opportunity of e-classroom. For that, different strategies had been applied like door-to-door question paper and answer sheet distribution, activity submission, etc; to keep all the students engaged in the system. After two years, most of the educational institutions are open and they are back to their usual form but with a lot of changes. The adopted technology in the education sector at the time of the pandemic may leave a long-lasting impression that will become an integral part of the system even in traditional classrooms.

Mental Health of the Students: School routines are important coping mechanisms for young people. When schools are closed, they lose an anchor in life. Students receive mental support from teachers and peers, such closures mean a lack of access to the resources they usually have through schools. Children belonging to privileged families have access to all learning materials but they are suffering from mental health issues due to their absences from the actual classroom. Parents were continually addressing issues such as depression and anxiety during the quarantine period with eating disorders. With the assistance of technology, virtual group work, and activity with parents were organized to reduce the mental stress of the students. Many national seminars were organized by the Government and NGOs to inform the parents and teachers about the mental health of the students at the time of lockdown and how to deal with that. Now, a major responsibility is to the teachers. It is challenging to recover them from their previous state of mind and to be a mental guide. Students need to familiarise themselves and sustained support is necessary to help them readjust and catch up after the pandemic. Schools must enable all children to return to school by providing a supportive learning environment to recover from their mental illness to create a better future.

Assessment and Performance Test: The unpreparedness of the teachers and the management of digital education lead to the unorganised assessment of the students. To continue the education with minimum interruption, it was mandatory to assess the performance of the students even at the time of the pandemic but the lack of training of teachers in technology made it difficult to assess students and their performance. The emergence of various educational Apps and Software made the work of teachers easier and recovered the teachers from their disrupted assessment process. Different assessment strategies have been tried and tested at the beginning of the lockdown. There were various methods employed by different organisations in order to streamline the education system to adapt to the new standard. Google classroom, MCQ-based tests, Open Book Assessment, and Project-Based Learning became vital tools for assessments. Now, students are acquainted with the new system and assessment technology. In a post-pandemic situation, after two years, when they are back in their classroom; the paper-pen test may become heavy for them due to the lack of habit of writing.

Financial instability and education system: The fall of the Indian economy due to the pandemic has affected everyone and the condition is worst in marginalised groups. It is important to provide support to this marginalised group and for the welfare of their education. The National Education Policy 2020, released by the Union government in July 2020, has also emphasised the importance of online education, blended with the traditional model. The Union government is banking hugely on the Bharatnet project, which aims to provide broadband to 250,000-gram panchayats in the country through the optic fiber to improve connectivity. Broadband connectivity in gram panchayats was expected to help rural schools provide online education to students who did not have internet access at home. Besides building the digital infrastructure, training is supposed to be given to the teachers to use the system to provide authentic and seamless education to the students. Priority must be given to the marginalised group to recover the disrupted system for the entire education sector. Many parents have owned a mobile phone just for the sake of a child's education. Children are back to school in their own traditional method of learning but it showed that parents did their best to recover their children's education. On the contrary, the drop-out number is not less. At the time of financial instability, students started working for the financial support of their families. It is quite tough to bring them to school in a post-pandemic situation. Due to the lack of access to digital modes of learning, many students discontinued. Now, they are not motivated to join the classroom anymore. It is challenging to recover them from their permanent loss.

Higher education and quality of education- According to UNESCO, higher education institutions (HEIs) were closed completely in 185 countries in April 2020, affecting more than 1,000 million learners around the globe (Marinoni et al., 2020). Especially, for higher studies many students change their places, states even countries to get the best education system in order to achieve their desired career. At the peak time of career-making, this pandemic changed the game of life. Few handled smartly and survived into the system, whereas many got out of the track. Most students were sent from their universities and colleges back to their homes for safety and protection. The unpreparedness of the higher education system caused havoc to the students. To recover the disruptive system various innovations emerged. The lecture-based classroom was easy to replace with a virtual classroom but teaching different skills to the students and practical classroom replacement was the most challenging part of the higher education by maintaining the quality of education. Due to the lack of IT infrastructure and skills, proper training and the creation of skilled personnel in the technical education system were beyond reach. In a country like India, even in the post-pandemic period, it is not possible to bring a huge change in the infrastructure of the colleges and universities to meet the demand of the time but yes, we are all involved in a digital world, and the phenomenon of online learning is here to stay. After two years the paradigm shift has occurred in university education but online teaching has gained relevance and the maintenance of the quality of education is still an ongoing process.

Challenges to the teachers

Students are habituated with online examinations and lost the habit of reading and memorization. Getting back into the groove of writing and taking notes is a difficult task. Students lost personal touch with the textbooks and being out of practice, is a struggle for children. They lag behind on work and time-management skills would need to be developed in order to finish hand-written exams on time. Besides the completion of the syllabus, teaching various skills at the same time is challenging for teachers in post-pandemic situations. Though the classes were conducted at the time of the pandemic, only content knowledge was delivered to the students. Now, after two years, with the reopening of schools, teachers are deliberately trying to bring the students back on track. During the lockdown, continuing the education system became the main target of teaching. Eventually, teachers-students-parents adopted the new method of teaching for the welfare of the students. Switching again to the traditional classroom is tough for the students if they do not get psychological support from the teachers. As countries seek to recover learning losses and build education sectors back better, teachers are playing a critical role. They are prepared, supported, and empowered to lead education recovery efforts. Teachers struggled themselves with technology at the time of complete lockdown to recover from the disrupted education system and in a post-pandemic situation, the duty is given to teachers to regenerate the education system once again with their magical wand.

Conclusion

Though Covid-19 has disrupted the education system, we can look at this moment as an opportunity for change. This transition was not possible but the pandemic directed us towards digitalization. The pandemic has also uncovered technology's potential and limitations – in supporting quality education for all. Technology can play a critical role in helping teachers to assess learning loss, track progress, develop remedial planning, and teach at the right level.

In the name of recovery from disruption, the education system can be reformed with proper initiative and measures for the betterment of future generations. The post-pandemic can be a blessing to the education system. Attending a physical classroom has reduced the screen time of the students but no one can completely stop the children from accessing the device. Once everyone is embracing technology, it is wise to utilize it in the correct way. When knowledge needs to be imparted; various strategies will be helpful to balance the mental health of the students and bring them into the system slowly but swiftly.

Bibliography

Pratap, H. ., & Singh, R. . (2021). Review on the New Education System after COVID-19 Pandemic. *NOLEGEIN- Journal of Information Technology &Amp; Management*, 4(1). Retrieved from https://mbajournals.in/index.php/JoITM/article/view/668

Dar, S. Ahmad & Lone, N.Ahmad (2021). *Impact of Covid-19 on Education in India. The Journal of Indian Art History Congress, 26* (2) *(XIV):2020-21.* 1-47. Retrieved from https://guides.library.uq.edu.au/referencing/apa6/journal-article

Kamal, T. and Illiyan, A. (2021). *School teachers' perception and challenges towards online teaching during COVID-19 pandemic in India: an econometric analysis. Asian Association of Open Universities Journal,*16, (3), 311-325. Retrieved from https://www.emerald.com/insight/content/doi/10.1108/AAOUJ-10-2021-0122/full/html

Babbar, M & Gupta,T. (2021). *Response of educational institutions to COVID-19 pandemic: An inter-country comparison. Sage Journals,*20 (4), 469-491. Retrieved from https://journals.sagepub.com/doi/pdf/10.1177/14782103211021937

Govindarajan, V.and Srivastava, A. (2020). *What the Shift to Virtual Learning Could Mean for the Future of Higher Education. Harvard Business Review.* Retrieved from https://guides.library.uq.edu.au/referencing/apa6/webpage

Jensen, T. (2019). *Higher Education in the Digital Era: The Current State of Transformation Around the World.* International Association of Universities. Retrieved from https://www.iau-aiu.net/IMG/pdf/

technology_report_2019.pdf

Marinoni, G., Van't Land, H., and Jensen, T. (2020). *The Impact of Covid-19 on Higher Education Around the World. IAU Global Survey Report.* Retrieved from https://www.iau-aiu.net/IMG/pdf/iau_covid19_and_he_survey_report_final_may_2020.pdf

BharatNet Scheme 2022: Application Form, Features & Tariff Details. (2022). Retrieved from https://pmmodiyojana.in/bharatnet-scheme/

MENTAL HEALTH AND WELL-BEING OF ADOLESCENT LEARNER: WAYS TO SUPPORT MENTAL HEALTH OF THE ADOLESCENT LEARNER

Dr. Shobha V. Kalebag Dr. Pratibha Rajaram Dabhade***

** Professor,Mahavir Mahavidyalaya, Kolhapur, Maharashtra.(India)*

*** Asst. Professor, MIT Saint Dnyaneshwar B. Ed. College, Alandi, Pune, Maharashtra.(India)*

ABSTRACT

Mental health is one dimension of health. Mental health is not mere absence of mental illness. A mentally healthy person is one who is free from internal conflicts. Adolescence is a unique and formative time. It is a crucial period for developing social and emotional habits important for mental well-being.

Multiple factors affect mental health. The more risk factors adolescents are exposed to, the greater the potential impact on their mental health. Factors that can contribute to stress during adolescence include exposure to adversity, pressure to conform with peers and exploration of identity. Media influence and gender norms can exacerbate the disparity between an adolescent's lived reality and their perceptions or aspirations for the future. Other important determinants include the quality of their home life and relationships with peers. Violence, harsh parenting and severe and socioeconomic problems are recognized risks to mental health. So, in the present scenario importance should be given to mental health and well-being of the adolescent learner.

There are different ways to support mental health of the adolescent learner. The ways are mental health awareness, caring and *supportive* relationships in *schools, healthy f*amily relationships and support, good relationship with peers, understanding the responsibility of social media, Developing problem-solving, and interpersonal skills and ability to cope with emotions, counselling, development of appropriate And accessible content by the industry etc.

KEY WORDS

Mental Health, Well-being, Adolescent Learner, Ways to support Mental Health

INTRODUCTION

Health is a common theme in most cultures. The oldest definition of health is "absence of disease". But according to WHO (1946) "Health is a state of complete physical, mental, and social well-being and not merely the absence of disease or infirmity."

Mental health is one dimension of health. Mental health is not mere absence of mental illness. A mentally healthy person is one who is free from internal conflicts. Control of emotions, sensitive to the needs of others, confidence in one's own abilities. A person is mentally healthy if he or she is relaxed and free from any worries.

According to the WHO, "Mental health is a state of **well-being** in which an individual realizes his or her own abilities, can cope with the normal stresses of life, can work productively, and is able to make a contribution to his or her community." Relationships, a sense of connection to peer groups and our personal sense of worth, physical health and motivation could lead to us developing a mental health condition such as anxiety, depression, substance misuse.

Mental health is a positive concept related to the social and emotional well-being of people and communities. The concept relates to the enjoyment of life, ability to cope with stress and sadness, the fulfillment of goals and potential, and a sense of connection to others. Mental health is about wellness rather than illness and is not merely the absence of a mental health condition. Like physical health, mental health is not fixed.

ADOLESCENT LEARNER

Adolescence is a distinct stage that marks the transition between childhood and adulthood. Psychologist Jean Piaget described adolescence as the period during which individuals' cognitive abilities fully mature. According to him, the transition from late childhood to adolescence is marked by the attainment of formal operational thought, the hallmark of which is abstract reasoning. Advances in the field of neuroscience have shown that the frontal cortex changes dramatically during adolescence. It is this part of the brain that controls higher-level cognitive processes such as planning, meta-cognition, and multitasking. Adolescent learners thrive in school environments that acknowledge and support their growing desire for autonomy, peer interaction, and abstract cognitive thinking, as well as the increasing salience of identity-related issues and romantic relationships. (Seel, 2012).

IMPORTANCE OF MENTAL HEALTH AND WELL-BEING OF THE ADOLESCENT LEARNER IN THE PRESENT SCENARIO

Adolescence is a unique and formative time. Physical, emotional and social changes, including exposure to poverty, abuse, or violence, can make adolescents vulnerable to mental health problems. Protecting adolescents from adversity, promoting socio-emotional learning and psychological well-being, and ensuring access to mental health care are critical for their health and well-being during adolescence and adulthood. Globally, it is estimated that (14%) 10-19 year-old experience mental health conditions, yet these remain largely unrecognized and untreated.

Adolescents with mental health conditions are particularly vulnerable to social exclusion, discrimination, stigma (affecting readiness to seek help), educational difficulties, risk-taking behaviours, physical ill-health and human rights violations. Adolescence is a crucial period for developing social and emotional habits important for mental well-being. These include adopting healthy sleep patterns; exercising regularly; developing coping, problem-solving, and interpersonal skills; and learning to manage emotions. Protective and supportive environments in the family, at school and in the wider community are important.

Multiple factors affect mental health. The more risk factors adolescents are exposed to, the greater the potential impact on their mental health. Factors that can contribute to stress during adolescence include exposure to adversity, pressure to conform with peers and exploration of identity. Media influence and gender norms can exacerbate the disparity between an adolescent's lived reality and their perceptions or aspirations for the future. Other important determinants include the quality of their home life and relationships with peers. Violence (especially sexual violence and bullying), harsh parenting and severe and socioeconomic problems are recognized risks to mental health.

Some adolescents are at greater risk of mental health conditions due to their living conditions, stigma, discrimination or exclusion, or lack of access to quality support and services. These include adolescents living in humanitarian and fragile settings; adolescents with chronic illness, autism spectrum disorder, an intellectual disability or other neurological condition; pregnant adolescents, adolescent parents, or those in early or forced marriages; orphans; and adolescents from minority ethnic or sexual backgrounds or other discriminated groups.

Almost half of the world is connected to the internet, and in countries that are members of the Organization for Economic Co-operation and Development (OECD) almost everyone is online (Echazarra, 2018[1]). For adolescents today, being online and using social media have become an integral part of their lives. In 2015, a typical 15-year-old from a country that is a member of the OECD had been using the internet since age 10 and spent more than two hours every weekday online after school, and more than three hours on a weekend day.

Half of all mental illnesses begin by the age of 14 and three-quarters by mid-20s (Kessler et al., 2007[10]), with anxiety and personality disorders sometimes beginning around age 11 (OECD, 2012[11]). Parents are concerned that young people are spending too much time in front of screens. Greater social media use is associated with poorer sleep and poorer mental health. Some other factors also show great influence on mental health and well-being of the adolescent learner. Factors are lack of caring and supportive relationships, support from family and peers, unawareness about digital use and risk, gender norms and intensification, lack of problem solving and interpersonal skills etc. So, in the present scenario importance should be given to mental health and well-being of the adolescent learner.

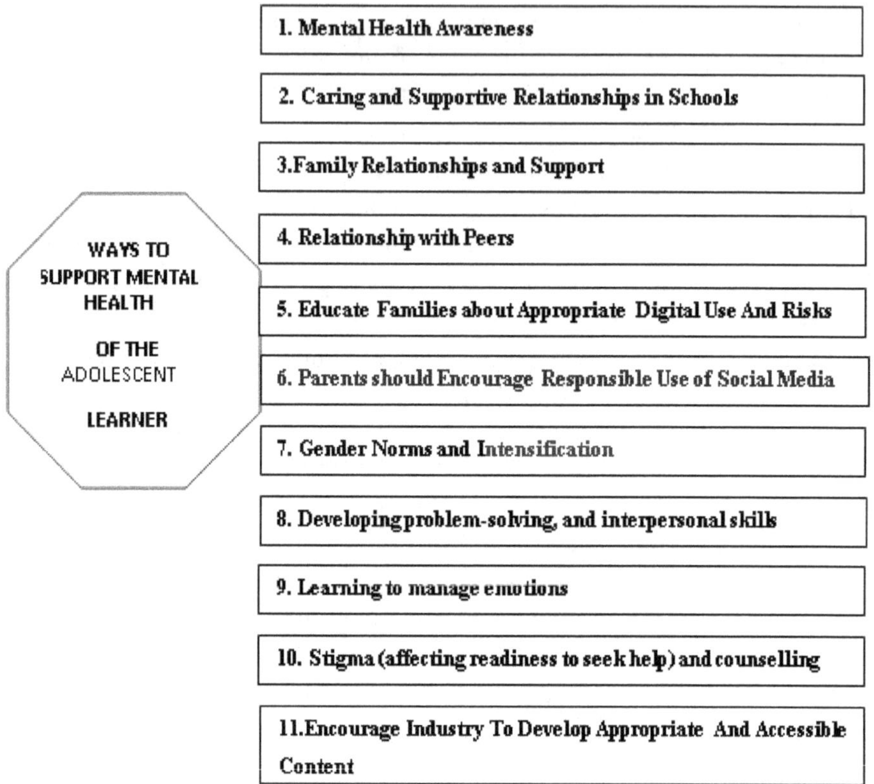

WAYS TO SUPPORT MENTAL HEALTH OF THE ADOLESCENT

Mental health of the adolescent learner can be supported by using following ways.

1. Mental Health Awareness

Mental health education is a mandatory aspect of all schools, teachers and administrators can work to promote awareness with their students. Teachers and students should be provided with ways to recognize signs of developing mental health problems, and there should be opportunities around the awareness and management of mental health crises, including the risk of suicide or self-harm. Further, instruction should address the relationship between mental health, substance abuse, and other negative coping behaviors, as well as the negative impact of stigma and cultural attitudes toward mental illness.

Because teens spend most of their day at school, it just makes sense to have mental health awareness and education become part of the curriculum. When we empower students with knowledge, and encourage dialogue, students will be able to get the help they need.

2. Caring and *Supportive* Relationships in *Schools*

Caring and *supportive* relationships in *schools* can help prevent a host of negative outcomes for children, including behavior problems. When students feel supported and cared for in their school environments, they are less likely to abuse substances, to become involved in violence, and to participate in other problematic behaviors. These students are also more likely to develop positive attitudes toward themselves and prosocial attitudes and behaviors toward others. When schools promote students' sense of connectedness, belonging, and community, they facilitate positive outcomes.

1. Family Relationships and Support

An increasing body of research demonstrates that negative family relationships can cause stress, impact mental health. Research has demonstrated that non-supportive families can detract from someone's mental health and or cause a mental illness to worsen. Most of the care that mental health sufferers often rely on is from family, so when family members deny this support, the recovery process can be negatively affected. Family relationships and support plays an important role in maintaining mental health of the adolescent learner.

3. Relationship with Peers

Peer relationships are associated with mental health disorders during adolescence. From a developmental perspective, the family plays a central role in the life of a child. However, in early adolescence the influence of peer relationships on social and emotional outcomes intensifies (Somerville, 2013) and these relationships become one of the key factors in shaping and directing young people's psychological development (Barnes et al., 2007). Evidence from cognitive neuroscience suggests that this period may be critical for the maturation of complex socio-emotional and cognitive skills that influence later mental health outcomes. So, schools and teachers should plan group activities in such a way that develops healthy relationships between adolescents with their peers.

4. Educate Families about Appropriate Digital Use And Risks

By developing digital knowledge and confidence, parents and carers can actively engage with technology and model constructive and balanced digital habits (Blum-Ross and Livingstone, 2016[32]). Any approach should account for the differences in parents' media proficiency, which is influenced by socioeconomic status, educational background and family structure (Nikken and Opree, 2018[33]). Governments should promote parental controls for different devices, as well as encourage co-viewing of content with children to help children understand what they are seeing and apply it to the world around them. In Germany, education is provided to parents about possible risks of online activities; while in Japan, legislation has funded increased education on appropriate internet use and promoted internet filtering and monitoring to parents (King et al., 2018[34]). To provide families with helpful guidance, there is a need for further research and improved measurement to address the lack of comparable data on children's mental health and wellbeing, as well as their internet and social media use, what content they are viewing and how they are interacting with it. There is a particular need for research covering primary school-aged or younger children, as children are utilising digital technologies at ever-younger ages (Hooft Graafland, 2018[35]).

4. Parents should Encourage Responsible Use of Social Media

Parents of adolescents should encourage responsible use of social media and limit some of its negative effects. Consider following tips:

a. **Set reasonable limits:**Parents should talk with their adolescent children about how to avoid letting social media interfere with their activities, sleep, meals or homework. Also encourage a bedtime routine that avoids electronic media use, and keep cellphones and tablets out of their bedrooms. Set an example by following these rules by them.

b. **Monitor adolescents accounts:** Let adolescent children know that their parents regularly check their social media accounts. They might aim to do so once a week or more. Make sure you follow through.

c. **Explain what's not OK:.** Discourage adolescent children from gossiping, spreading rumors, bullying or damaging someone's reputation — online or otherwise. Talk with them about what is appropriate and safe to share on social media.

d. **Encourage face-to-face contact with friends:** This is particularly important for adolescent children vulnerable to social anxiety disorder.

e. **Talk about social media:** Parents should talk about their own social media habits. They can ask their adolescent how they are using social media and how it makes him or her feel. Remind their children that social media is full of unrealistic images.

5. Gender Norms and Intensification

Gender norms are ideas about how women and men should be and act. Gender intensification, an increased pressure for adolescents to conform to culturally sanctioned gender roles, has been posited as an explanation for the emergence of the gender difference in depression. Whether we like it or not, culture dictates many of the expectations we have for boys and girls, men and women. We all have our own concepts of masculinity and femininity, and how those should be manifested.

Women are typically viewed as more emotional, sensitive, and dependent. Men, on the other hand, are often told to act stronger, less vulnerable, and less emotional. While there may be some truth behind these stereotypes, gender-based expectations for how people should behave can actually be harmful, especially when it comes to mental health.

We cannot change the culture. But still there are many gender stereotypes relating to skills, academic potential, and careers, which we can all perpetuate without meaning to. They can have a real influence on how girls and boys in adolescent stage feel about their own abilities.Various school programme help teachers, parents and students to overcome stereotypes and also changes students' attitudes and aspirations.

6. Developing problem-solving, and interpersonal skills

Everybody needs to solve problems every day and also need interpersonal skills. But we're not born with these skills. We have to develop them. In adolescent children problem solving and interpersonal skills should be developed. Here the role of the parents, teachers and schools are very important.

7. Learning to manage emotions

Emotional health allows working productively and coping with the stresses of everyday life. It can help us to realize our full potential. By using following ways adolescent children can improve or maintain good emotional health.

a. **Be aware of your emotions and reactions** - Notice what in your life makes you sad, frustrated, or angry. Try to address or change those things.

b. **Express your feelings in appropriate ways** - Let people close to you know when something is bothering you. Keeping feelings of sadness or anger inside adds to stress. It can cause problems in your relationships and at school.

c. **Think before you act** - Give yourself time to think and be calm before you say or do something you might regret.

d. **Manage stress.** Learn relaxation methods to cope with stress. These could include deep breathing, meditation, and exercise.

e. **Strive for balance** - Find a healthy balance between work and play, and between activity and rest. Make time for things you enjoy. Focus on positive things in your life.

f. **Take care of your physical health** – There is a strong association between physical and mental health. Physical exercise is associated with improved psychological well-being for adolescents. The World Health Organization recommendation is for an hour of moderate to vigorous exercise every day for adolescents, in addition to whatever they do in school- that means activity that gets them sweating and breathing hard. But many adolescents don't exercise anywhere near that much. They should get healthy meals, and enough sleep.

g. **Connect with others** - Make a lunch date, join a group, and say hi to strangers. We need positive connections with other people.

h. **Find purpose and meaning** - Figure out what's important to you in life, and focus on that. This could be your work, your family, volunteering, caregiving, or something else. Spend your time doing what feels meaningful to you.

a. **Stay positive** - Focus on the good things in your life. Forgive yourself for making mistakes and forgive others. Spend time with healthy, positive people.

8. **Stigma (affecting readiness to seek help) and counselling**

The high levels of stigma associated with mental illness make it difficult for adolescent children struggling to seek treatment. Often they fear being labelled as "crazy" and being ostracized if their friends become aware they have a mental illness. This fear of being "found out" causes them to avoid seeking treatment, fail to take medications, isolate, and lose self-esteem. In this situation parents should play an important role. As per the need, parents can do counselling or they can take help of a professional counsellor.

9. Encourage Industry To Develop Appropriate And Accessible Content

Governments should encourage online broadcasters, digital developers and entrepreneurs to produce technology that fits a child's development via 'age-appropriate' content, as well as ensure inappropriate content is not accessible. Companies are starting to respond to these calls, enabling easy-to-use safety features that are accessible to those with basic digital literacy (Livingstone et al., 2014[28]), with Microsoft, Sony, and Nintendo providing online guides and video demonstrations on setting time limits and content restrictions on their gaming systems (King et al., 2018[34]). Apps are now available to help limit children and young people's screen time and track their online activity, whether tracking and setting limits on daily social media usage via Moment; comparing screen usage to those the same age and gender using antisocial, or using Space and App Detox to set screen locks and time use goals. In response to this demand, Google, Apple, Facebook and Instagram are also introducing new tools. For users to monitor daily use and set screen time limits. While the availability of these tools is welcome, there is no evidence yet that demonstrates these tools reduce screen time on their own, although they could act as an additional factor in encouraging children to moderate their time online.

CONCLUSION

Protecting adolescents from adversity, promoting socio-emotional learning and psychological well-being, and ensuring access to mental health care are critical for their health and well-being during adolescence and adulthood. In this technological age, greater social media use is associated with poorer sleep and poorer mental health. Some other factors also show great influence on mental health and well-being of the adolescent learner. Factors are lack of caring and supportive relationships, support from family and peers, unawareness about digital use and risk, gender norms and intensification, lack of problem solving and interpersonal skills etc. So, in the present scenario importance should be given to mental health and well-being of the adolescent learner. The ways given in this article will support the mental health and well-being of adolescent learners.

WEBLIOGRAPHY

https://www.education.vic.gov.au/school/teachers/health/mentalhealth/Pages/promoting-mental-health.aspx

https://www.coe.int/en/web/campaign-free-to-speak-safe-to-learn/improving-well-being-at-school

https://www.unicef.org/coronavirus/8-teacher-tips-student-mental-health

http://www.ibe.unesco.org/en/glossary-curriculum-terminology/a/adolescent-learners

https://www.who.int/news-room/fact-sheets/detail/adolescent-mental-health

https://www.wgu.edu/heyteach/article/importance-mental-health-awareness-schools1810.html

https://safesupportivelearning.ed.gov/training-technical-assistance/education-level/early-learning/protective-factors

https://www.oecd.org/els/health-systems/Children-and-Young-People-Mental-Health-in-the-Digital-Age.pdf

https://www.pinerest.org/newsroom/articles/mental-illness-stigma-keeps-people-from-seeking-help-blog/

https://www.frontiersin.org/articles/10.3389/fpsyg.2021.589403/full

https://bold.expert/encouraging-gender-equality-in-schools/?gclid=Cj0KCQjwr-SSBhC9ARIsANhzu14sCK0gISBa2hNwGtJ2_66NUFnbqJAgOaeMSI9WnN-p_HmOQVNI9eAaAs-qEALw_wcB

https://www.nytimes.com/2020/03/02/well/family/the-benefits-of-exercise-for-childrens-mental-health.html

CHAPTER FIFTEEN

Reform of Secondary Education in India after COVID-19

Subhamita Paul M.Ed(Burdwan University)

Abstract:

The sudden closure of schools, colleges and universities left very little time for the system to prepare a strategy and transition to distance learning. To broaden the outreach of online or digital education and remote learning and ensure its accessibility to all students in all sectors of society. Still, this method is the initial evolving phase in the country. MHRD takes initiatives for digital education. There were no limitations as to the place of learning or studying. Through the mode of digital education, learning can be made more participative and collaborative between the students and teachers. Digital learning is the best medium for students to study as well as play through interactive worksheets and activities. The National Education Policy, 2020 focuses on improving the standard of education through various measures such as introducing new pedagogical and curricular structure, early childhood care and education, development of knowledge, a transformation evaluation system for student development, and experiential and skilful learning.

Keywords: COVID-19, digital education, learning gap.

INTRODUCTION:

The COVID-19 crisis has keenly affected the education system all over the world. Schools have been fully closed during the pandemic. In response to this crisis, most countries have pursued online learning. As a result, the education system has changed awfully with the remarkable rise of e-learning, whereby teaching is undertaken remotely and on digital platforms. Online learning is beneficial in several ways but it has certain limitations too. In India, a large no of the population cannot afford smartphones. There is less internet availability in many areas. Online learning has taken a huge toll on the mental and physical health of students as well as their teachers.

Students were facing many health issues i.e. headaches, and eyesight problems. Education hampers are one of the biggest global threats to recovery from COVID-19. "we must continue to sound the alarm on the crisis in education and ensure that policymakers have clear evidence for how to recover the catastrophic learning and losses and prevent a lost generation" said Jaime Saavedra, Panel member and Global Director for Education at the World Bank. UNICEF, UNESCO and World Bank have joined together to launch Mission Recovery Education 2021 focusing on three prime concerns:

- All children and youth are back in school and accept the tailored services needed to meet their learning, health, psychosocial wellbeing and other needs.
- Students receive productive remedial learning to retrieve learning losses.
- All teachers are prepared and held up to address learning losses among their students and to incorporate digital technology into their teaching.

Department-related parliamentary standing committee on Education, Women, Children, Youth and Sports (5th August 2021) decided to examine in detail the subject "Plans to Bridge the Learning Gap caused due to School Lockdown as well as Review of Online and Offline instructions and examinations and plans for re-opening of Schools." UNICEF informed the Committee of some significant findings of the study conducted by them, as follows:

- 1.5 million schools/1.37 million AWC closed disrupting the education of over 286 million students;
- Only 24% of households have access to the internet and only 61. of household sold own a smartphone;
- 40% of students had not accessed any remote learning.
- Rural students were 10% less likely to have accessed remote learning than their urban peers;
- Children faced psychosocial challenges to school closures which affected learning.

Strategies for strengthening education:
1) **Power up teachers:**

Teachers are the main backbone of education. Countries around the world shift to re-opening to recover education, teachers who will be on the front lines of this challenging effort. Ensuring adequate funding for high-quality and effective professional development experiences for all teachers that support their development and success, must be a priority that goes hand-in-hand as to return students and teachers to classrooms. For this purpose, The World Bank started a new program COACH that seeks to build and strengthens skills. The Prime Minister of India launched "Vidyanjali 2.0" is like a platform for the country's resolve of "Sabkha Prays' with 'Sabkha Shaath, Sabkha Vikas, Sabkha Vishwas." In this society, many private sectors have to come forward and contribute to increasing the quality of education in government schools. There are several initiatives are taken by Govt. of India for teacher's improvement-

a) **NISHTHA (National Initiative for School Heads and Teachers for Their Holistic Advancement) ONLINE**: Giving financial support up to Rs 1000 per teacher for procuring pen drives, the printing of modules and a high-speed data pack have been provided.

b) **Special capacity building of teachers on how to conduct online classes:** CIET-NCERT organised a series of webinars for the enrichment and professional development of teachers and teacher educators. Till 25th February 2021, about 265 episodes have been conducted and broadcasted through NCERT's official YouTube channel, PM e-VIDYA DTH TV channels.

c) CBSE has **mapped the learning outcomes** for all subjects and all grades. Mapping shows how the current requirements of any programme support the achievement of learning outcome goals. Mapped learning outcomes to the curriculum are available at http://cbseacademic.nic.in/web_material//Manuals/TeachersResource_LODoc.pdf

2) **Changing of assessment:**

Learning of students previously is measured by only summative and formative methods. We can also ask students to reflect and report on their learning. Asking students to rate their knowledge about a topic after taking admission in a course as compared to what they believe they knew before taking admission is an example. With the adoption of **Sustainable Development Goals 2030** by India, CBSE introduced the **School Quality Assessment and Assurance Framework (SQAAF).**

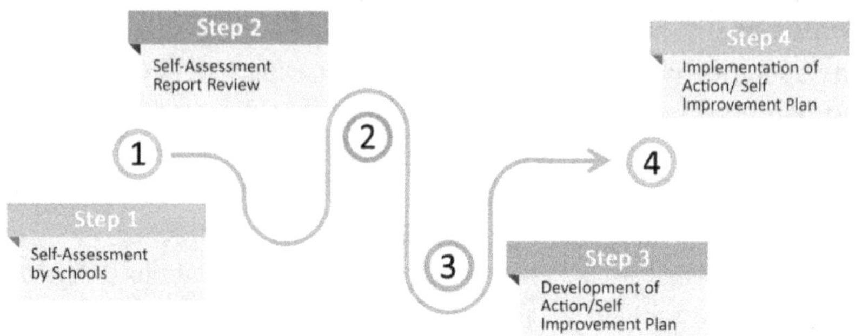

Process of SQAA Framework

3) Different scholarships programmes:

The Coronavirus Aid, Relief, and Economic Security (CARES) Act was enacted by U.S. Congress in March 2020 to blunt the economic damage during COVID-19. As a part of that law and other pieces of legislation passed by Congress, the **Higher Education Emergency Relief Fund (HEERF)**, was established. These grants can be used to cover many needs of needy students like the cost of course materials, food, and hand-health care. Many students lost their parents in the pandemic situation, forced to leave their study for the joblessness of their parents, many of whom are being forced to drop out of schools or colleges for the same. Three major scholarship programmes in India for them are introduced. These are-

a) **Kotak Shiksha Nidhi** for continuity of their education from class 1 to diploma and graduate level courses.

b) **HDFC Bank Parivartan's** COVID Crisis Support Scholarship Programme 2021 aims to support students who are studying in class 1 to a post-graduation level to continue their education.

c) **Digital Bharati COVID Scholarship 2021-22 invites** applications from children who are left vulnerable with very little or no financial support for their further education owing to a COVID-led crisis in their family.

4) Strengthen digital education:

The Ministry of Human Resource Development released **PRAGYATA** guidelines on Digital Education, to improve online education and ensure the safety and academic welfare of the students.

The period of classes as per the PRAGYATA guidelines should be as follows:

DIVISION	SCREEN TIME FOR STUDENTS
Pre-primary students	Not more than 30 minutes a day
Classes 1-8	Not more than 2 online sessions per day, : minutes each as decided by states/UTC
Classes 9-12	Maximum four sessions per day, 30-45 m each as decided by states/UTC

NCERT develops an **Alternative Academic Calendar** for all stages of school education to engage students meaningfully during their stay at home due to COVID-19 through educational activities at home. It is available at https://ncert.nic.in/alternative-academic-calender.php

To strengthen digital learning and make the Atma Nirbhar Bharat Programme govt. unifies all efforts related to digital education to enable multi-mode access to education. For that purpose, the PM e Vidya programme started. It has the following components:

DIKSHA- Digital Infrastructure for Knowledge Sharing. One nation, One digital education platform. It has QR-coded textbooks for students and teachers. 1140 JNV teachers were required to create E-content for DIKSHA. KVS has uploaded and published creative and critical thinking practice (CCT) items and videos on Mathematics and Science.

SWAYAM PRABHA- One class, one TV channel. It has a total of 34 channels are devoted to telecasting high-quality educational programmes.

CHANNEL	TIME FOR A FRESH SLOT	REPEAT	DURATION
Class 1to 10	2hrs	11 times	30 mints
Class 11 to 12	3hrs	8 times	60mints

E-CONTENT FOR OPEN SCHOOL BY NIOS: National Institute of Open Schooling (NIOS) has also started imparting daily 8 hrs live programmes of 4 hrs each on PM eVidya channels. They telecast programmes for secondary and senior secondary levels on Swayam Prabha- Panini (Secondary) and

Sharda (Senior Secondary) channels including holidays also.

EXTENSIVE USE OF RADIO, COMMUNITY RADIO AND PODCAST: A podcast called Shikshavani by CBSE is being effectively used by learners of grades 9 to 12. Radio broadcasting is being used for children in remote areas who are not able to use mobile phones and the Internet.

OLABS: Practical-related e-content has been made available for senior students. There are interactive simulations, animations and lab videos. These are available at http://www.olabs.edu.in/

NATIONAL DIGITAL ONLINE LIBRARY: It is a virtual repository of learning resources and provides a host of services for the learner community. It contains more than 50 million resources.

E-PATHSHALA: This portal and mobile apps are a storehouse of audio, videos, epubs, flipbooks etc. Students can be accessed through laptops, desktops, tablets and mobile phones. Resources are ready to use in Hindi, English and Urdu.

Aside from the above, the NCERT and CBSE also prepared many contents and uploaded it on DIKSHA:

- Comic books.
- Practice book on Mathematical literacy.
- Cyber Safety and Cyberbullying. This handbook is available at: http://cbseacademic.nic.in/web_material/Manuals/ Cyber_Safety_Manual.pdf

- Several quiz competitions- "Punnet Sagar Abhiyan" was launched in December 2021 by NCC. Poshan Maah 2022, Swaraj Quiz, Khel aur Ban quiz, Swachh Sagar Surakshit Sagar, Desh Ke Utsav Quiz. These are all available at http://quiz.mygov.in

During the lockdown, AICTE conducted 85 virtual programmes using the platforms of Microsoft, Webex, Zoom and Google. 18,000 faculty were trained in emerging technologies. AICTE also conducted 22 programmes on universal human values. To make up for the loss of academic time, the UP govt. had designed a separate module called "Samruddh" for accelerated and remedial learning.

WAY OF RECOVERY OF EDUCATION:

1) **Midday meal scheme:**

Andhra Pradesh, West Bengal, Karnataka, Kerala, and Chhattisgarh provide dry rations to the students. Whereas Bihar Govt. has initiated cash transfer to parents account for primary and upper primary students. The Odisha Govt. has started the GHARE GHARE ARUNIMA programme in coordination with UNICEF to provide a home-based curriculum for Anganwadi-going children who remain in houses due to the pandemic.

Height	Regularly eat MDM	Weight	Regularly eat MDM
Several stunted	0.070	Severely underweight	0.106
Stunted	0.086	Underweight	-0.028**
Average height	0.007**	Average weight	0.003**
Tall	-0.168	Overweight	0.033
Taller	0.005**	Obese	-0.114**

Source: Status Report- Government and private schools during COVID-19

The UN World Food Programme has been supporting governments to adapt their means programs during school closures. The loss of education caused by school closures smashes into the health and nutrition of children in the long term.

2) Reopening of schools:

Schools should be kept open by maintaining COVID protocols. Measures have included physical distancing by reducing class sizes and putting hand washing stations or mask-wearing. In some countries (France, Qatar, Estonia) COVID testing within schools has been possible. In Argentina, a website has been launched to monitor the COVID situation in schools. Many countries take steps to support learner and teacher well-being. For example, allocation of additional school counsellors (Japan), provision of hotlines to provide psychological support (Armenia) and specific school wellbeing policy (Canada). Schools should be at the heart of society, protected by us as a safe place for children to learn and be together. UNICEF in coordination with the Ministry of Education, culture and Research with national NGOs have been developing training materials for teachers in the context of school reopening. Initiatives for mental well-being and psychological support are taken by the Department of School Education and Literacy (DOSEL)-

a) **MANODARPAN** for psychological support to students (Schools/ Universities/Colleges/ Institutions), and teachers for Mental Health and

Emotional Wellbeing during the COVID outbreak and beyond. The webpage is available at: https://manodarpan.education.gov.in.

b) Mental health and well-being manuals are prepared by CBSE covering self-care, positivity, dealing with fear and anxiety, the importance of social support and staying connected. This manual is available at: http://cbse.nic.in/newsite/attach/CBSE%20MH%20Manual.pdf

c) Tele-counselling by CBSE related to pre-board exam, post-result period and students of residential schools.

d) CBSE partnered with FIT INDIA programme viz-Quiz, Freedom run, Yoga etc. through online and offline mood.

Department-related parliamentary standing committee on Education, Women, Children, Youth and Sports (5th August 2021) recommended the following:

a) Vaccine programmes for all students, teachers and allied staff so that school starts functioning normally.

b) Regular thermal screening at the time of the entry of students /teachers/staff. A sick room with essential facilities may be set up in each school.

c) Students belonging to economically weaker sections of society may be supplied hand sanitiser/facemasks at regular intervals etc.

3) **Tracking dropouts:**

Negative social (forced marriage and violence, adolescent pregnancy) and economic impacts are raising the risk of dropouts. For that reason, UNESCO has launched a campaign "Learning never stops" for girls during school closer. The figure for dropouts at the Secondary level was as high in India and some children have never been enrolled. The Ministry of Education has launched to track out-of-school children (missing children) on the **PRABANDHA** portal to facilitate State/UTs in uploading the data.

CONCLUSION:

During the pandemic children are learning to study from home or in open spaces, through devices, or even worksheets and with the help of volunteers and peers, due to the closure of schools, dropouts and out-of-school children have become a large area of concern. The Ministry of Education takes several interventions to help states and schools to extinguish the effects of the pandemic. We shifted to a substitute education mode but that was not attainable for all. Children belonging to the poor or even middle class were not able to arrange the required smartphones or get internet access for online learning. This situation also made it crystal clear that nothing can substitute schooling. The laboratory-based classes and the mathematics classes are very difficult to conduct in online mode. The providing of Aakash- a low-budget computer by the Government of India as a part of an initiative of e-learning improvement. Fortunately, NEP2020 has paid attention to this. At the same time, it cannot be ignored that online learning can be a useful mode through which students are not only taught content knowledge but also communication skills as well. Through the help of online machine learning and artificial intelligence, teachers can easily bridge the learning gap of our students. Union Budget 2022-23 could provide a significant stimulant to the education sector. The nodal Ministry for Education has received Rs.1,04,277 crore for 2022-23, 12% higher than the previous year's budget estimates. In 2021, "The Pradhan Mantri Poshan Shakti Nirman", a modified version of the existing Mid-Day Meal scheme was launched. To alleviate the impact of the pandemic, there is a vitally important need to have an emergency and appropriate strategy to secure a continuum of learning. We have taken a multi-faceted and comprehensive approach to ensure that children received suitable support.

References:

1) Chandra, Y. (2020, October 6). Online education during COVID-19: perception of academic stress and emotional intelligence coping strategies among college students. *Asian Education and Development Studies, 10*(2), 229–238. Retrieve from https://doi.org/10.1108/aeds-05-2020-0097

2) Ahmed, S., Taqi, H. M. M., Farabi, Y. I., Sarker, M., Ali, S. M., & Sankaranarayanan, B. (2021, April 9). Evaluation of Flexible Strategies to Manage the COVID-19 Pandemic in the Education Sector. *Global Journal of Flexible Systems Management, 22*(S2), 81–105. Retrieve from https://doi.org/10.1007/s40171-021-00267-9

3) Education Commission,2019. Save Our Future White paper: Averting an Education Catastrophe for the World's Children. Retrieve from http://saveourfuture.world/wp-content/uploads/2020/10/Averting-an-Education-Catastrophe-for-the-Worlds-Children_SOF_White-paper.pdf.

4) UNESCO, 2020. Retrieve from http://en.unesco.org/covid19/educationrespose

5) UNICEF, 2021. Effectiveness of digital learning solutions to improve educational outcomes. A review of the evidence. Working paper. Retrieve from https://www.unicef.org/documents/effectiveness-digital-learning-solutions-improve-educational-outcomes

CHAPTER SIXTEEN

ROLE OF ICT IN PERSONAL, SOCIAL, AND EDUCATIONAL EMPOWERMENT OF WOMEN

SUKANTA SAHA M. ED, Burdwan University

INTRODUCTION

If a person can realize himself properly then it can be said that his overall empowerment occurred. Empowerment is a process that helps individuals to develop their thoughts, unique Character, and act autonomously. Through this process the individual can lead his own life, can make his choice, and remove choice boundaries created by others. In a word, empowerment is about building trust and confidence in yourself and at the same time building yourself as a strong person. Empowerment of women means giving women their due share in all spheres of society. One of the main goals of women's empowerment is to create and provide equal and necessary opportunities for women in social, political, educational, health, spiritual, and other areas of life. Women's welfare, women's development, and women's empowerment are all interconnected elements that provide women an opportunity to change their life, taking own decisions, and have equal rights to participate in all activities in society.

Women are an integral part of society and women's empowerment is an essential element for the overall development of society and nation. The knowledge-based society of every country considers every person as its human resource. Therefore, an atmosphere of equal opportunities and empowerment is created in all these countries regardless of men and women. In an Indian knowledge-based society, the main objective of women's empowerment is to enhance women's skills and capabilities that make them useful in society and ensure their participation in economic and political spheres by freeing them from all the social and institutional restrictions placed on them.

Empowerment means giving them rights and allowing them to ask questions about everything in our society. If we follow the Nobel lecture by Malala Yosufzai, she asked some questions about girls' rights and opportunities- '' I am Amina. I am those 66 million girls who are deprived of education, and today I am not raising my voice, it is the voice of those 66 million girls. Sometimes people like to ask me why should girls go to school, why is it important for them. But I think the more important question is why should not they? Why should not they have this right to go to school?

In the issue of women's empowerment ICT is the most powerful tool. Even in the 21st century women are victims of social discrimination. Social screens and prejudices still exist in many societies. Most of which apply to women. Where women are forced to spend time at home. But with the use of ICT, they can easily know what is happening outside their home and around the world. At the same time, through ICT they can express their views about various social issues and overcome social barriers. Therefore, ICT should be seen as an important tool in the context of women's development in society. Research has already been done at the national and international levels on the role of ICT in enhancing women's empowerment. But a new direction can be seen, in how information and communication technology help in the Personal, Social, and educational empowerment of university-going women students (girl students). Considering this limited work, the current research will be a new addition to education.

LITERATURE REVIEW

- Beena (2015), in her thesis ''Empowerment of rural women through ICT education-A case study'', examines the impact of ICT on the empowerment of rural women. The research is concerned with the study of women empowerment and ICT education in rural areas of Jaipur districts. The research method used for the study was case study method. A purposive sampling area was chosen for the data collection. Both primary and secondary data were collected. 32 respondents were selected randomly from purposive areas. The major findings were, all (32) respondents accept that they getting helps from ICT for the improvement of their education, majority of respondents accept that ICT helps them in improve their confidence and self-efficiency.

- McLeod (2014), in his study "Community attitude and ICT intervention program for school girls" focuses on the importance of community attitudes toward ICT to the outcome of the digital Divas (DD) intervention program, run in secondary schools in Australia, from 2000-2012 l, is investigated. A survey method is used for collecting data. This study emphasizes the attitudinal changes of girl students who joined the DD program. And the result comes out, there are attitudinal changes among DD students after participating DD program. Inside DD students' attitude, community attitude also takes place in this program. The main objective of this thesis is to prove, that if girl's student involves in the ICT program, then there will be changes in their attitude.

- Mohapatra, s. (2014), in her research paper ''ICT and its impact on Women: A study in two districts of Odisha, aims at understanding the Impact of ICT on women in general. One main objective of this paper, the study and understand the use of ICTs by rural and urban women in the Khurda (Urban) and Ganjam (Rural) districts. The Nayapalli-6 area of the Khurda district and the Kanheipur area of the Ganjam district were selected as sample collection areas. Both primary and secondary data were collected. Snowball and simple random sampling techniques were used for data collection. 100 rural and 70 urban women were interviewed. Various findings were found. Urban women of Niyapalli- are more confident to use ICT than rural women of Kanheipur.

- Dinesh (2013), in his thesis "Role of Information Communication technologies for women empowerment: A Kerala Experience", assess the impact of economic and social enhancement of women workforce in Information and communication technologies (ICTs). Both primary and secondary data were collected, and three regions of Kerala were selected for the sampling area of this study. 310 working women in ICT units were interviewed. The judgment sampling method was used in this study. This study consists of various findings for the fulfillment of the objectives. It was found that ICTs jobs are contributing the women's empowerment. This study concluded that ICT-based initiatives empower women.

- The government of India ministry of women and child development (2013), published a report entitled "enhancing women's empowerment through information and communication technology: A report'', and this report was submitted by the voluntary association for people service (VAPS). Under this report VAPS developed a questionnaire entitled enhancing women empowerment through information and communication technology; 37 questions were prepared. 1st and 2nd questions were related to the basic and family information of respondents. And next 35 questions were related to the use of ICTs and empowerment through ICT. In this questionnaire, multiple types of questions were prepared, fill-in blanks, Yes/No, and open-ended questions.

- Purusothaman (2011), in her study "Role of ICT in the educational upliftment of women- Indian scenario", focuses on the need and significance of information and communication technologies in the educational sector. The main objective of this paper was to show the challenges of Indian students for effective use of ICT through action research in a workshop and try to show the changes among women students before and after the use of ICT training program. The response group was eight female students. Questionnaire methods were used for collecting data. Among various findings, one important finding was, after attending that workshop they earned more expertise in using various ICT tools than before attending the program.

Statement of the problem.

Based on the Review of Literature and emergence, the Statement of the Problem is defined as '' Role of ICT in personal, social, and educational empowerment women''.

Objectives of the Study

The basic objectives of the present study are given below:

- To study the personal, social, and educational empowerment of university women students through ICT.
- To compare the personal empowerment of science and arts stream university women students through ICT.
- To compare the social empowerment of science and arts stream university women students through ICT.
- To compare the educational empowerment of science and arts stream university women students through ICT.
- To find out the status of personal, social, and educational empowerment of university science stream women students through ICT separately in terms of %.
- To find out the status of personal, social, and educational empowerment of university arts stream women students through ICT separately in terms of %.

Hypotheses

To achieve the objectives of the study, the following hypotheses have been generated:

- Significant difference exists between the personal empowerment of science and arts stream university women students through ICT.
- Significant difference exists between the social empowerment of science and arts stream university women students through ICT.
- Significant difference exists between the educational empowerment of science and arts stream university women students through ICT.

Hypotheses in Null form

NH_1 : No significant difference exists between the personal empowerment of science and arts stream university women students through ICT.

NH_2 : No significant difference exists between the social empowerment of science and arts stream university women students through ICT.

NH_3 : No significant difference exists between the educational empowerment of science and arts stream university women students through ICT.

Consequences

C_1 Significant difference exists between the mean scores of personal empowerment of science and arts stream university women students through ICT.

C_2 Significant difference exists between the mean scores of social empowerment of science and arts stream university women students through ICT.

C_3 Significant difference exists between the mean scores of educational empowerment of science and arts stream university women students through ICT.

Delimitation of the study

- The study has been delimited to Burdwan university only.
- The study has been delimited to the Postgraduate (PG) academic level only.
- The study has been delimited to science and arts stream only.

Significance of the study

At present, we are realizing the role of ICT every step of the way. On other hand, the government and private sector in India has been an emphasis on women's empowerment by eliminating social inequalities. Somehow, both of them are related to education and human development.

In India where patriarchal society is still prevalent. Women are still living in society keeping many of their desires and reluctance secret. There have been many studies on ICT and women, ICT helps in the multifaceted empowerment of women. There is a need for more work or research on this which will increase the awareness of women as well as society. This needs to be discussed how ICT takes a role in the personal, social, and educational empowerment of women.

This study is being done keeping in mind the women students studying at Masters's level at Burdwan University. The study focuses on the status of the use of ICTs in the Personal, social, and educational empowerment of women. And it is being tried to see in which areas of empowerment they are using ICTs to empower themselves. Through the results of the study, the researcher hopes to contribute an important role in reflecting the three dimensions of women's empowerment and its enhancement through ICTs.

METHODOLOGY

Population:

For this study, all the women students doing post-graduate academic courses from Burdwan University were taken as a population.

Sample:

100 women students consisting of 40 science and 60 arts students doing post-graduate from Burdwan University were selected as sample.

Sampling Technique:

100 women students (40 from the science stream and 60 from the arts stream) doing the post-graduate from Burdwan University have been selected randomly.

Used Tool:

Women Empowerment through ICT Scale (WETIS), developed by Gupta and Bala (2018) was adapted for this study. Split-half reliability was found at .73

Statistical Techniques Used:

Mean, Median, Mode, Standard Deviation, Quartile, Skewness, and Kurtosis were calculated for personal, social, and educational empowerment of post-graduate science and arts University women students separately. The percentage was calculated to find out the status of empowerment of women university arts and science students through ICT. t-test was done to compare the different types of empowerment personal, social, and educational of science and arts University women students through ICT.

Results and Discussions

Determination of descriptive statistics regarding empowerment of Science- and Arts- University Women students'

	Science- Students' (N=40)			Arts- Students' (N=60)		
	Personal	Social	Educational	Personal	Social	Educational
Mean	43.12	36.75	43.7	38.58	39.25	37.8
Median	43.03	36.5	43.43	40.21	39.71	41
Mode	42.64	35.75	43	34.5	38.16	33.3
Standard Deviation	3.195	5.47	2.846	6.25	5.117	9.21
Quartile	2.475	4.6	1.94	3.585	3.15	6.305
Skewness	0.173	0.115	0.64	-2.855	-1.085	-6.36
Kurtosis	0.270	0.32	0.24	0.2508	0.257	0.239

Table 1: Descriptive statistics regarding the empowerment of Science- and Arts- Students' in respect of Personal, Social, and Educational Empowerment.

Determination of the status of empowerment of Science- and Arts- University Women students

		% BELOW AVERAGE	% AVERAGE	% ABOVE AVERAGE
PERSONAL	SCIENCE	22.5	55	22.5
	ARTS	21.67	78.33	0
SOCIAL	SCIENCE	15	60	25
	ARTS	21.68	51.66	26.66
EDUCATIONAL	SCIENCE	10	67.5	22.57
	ARTS	36.68	56.66	6.66

Table 2: Status of personal, social, and educational empowerment of Science- and Arts- University Women Students' in percentage.

From Table 2 it is clear that Science students are more empowered personally and educationally than their Arts counterparts. As there is sharp discrimination in above-average cases. But in the case of social empowerment, no such sharp discrimination is found.

Determination of the difference in personal empowerment of Science- and Arts- University students' through ICT.

GROUPS \ MEASURES	N	M	SD	SE_D	t	P
Science Personal	40	43.125	3.195			
				0.94	4.84	P< .01
Arts Personal	60	38.58	6.25			

Table 3: t- and p-value of the difference between mean scores in Personal Empowerment of Science- and Arts- Students' through ICT along with other relevant measures

Table 3 shows that the t-value between mean scores in personal empowerment of science- and arts- stream university women students are 4.84 which is significant at less than the .01 level.

So, a significant difference exists between the personal empowerment of science- and arts-stream university women students' through ICT confirming Hypothesis 1 i.e., ₐ Significant difference exists between personal empowerment of science and arts stream university women students' through ICT.

Determination of the difference in Social empowerment of Science- and Arts- University students' through ICT.

GROUPS \ MEASURES	N	M	SD	SE_D	t	P
Science Social	40	36.75	5.47			
				1.087	2.29	P< .05
Arts Social	60	39.25	5.11			

Table 4: t- and p-value of the difference between mean scores in Social Empowerment of science- and Arts- Students' through ICT along with other relevant measures

Table 4 shows that the t-value between mean scores in social empowerment of science- and arts- stream university women students' is 2.29 which is significant at less than the .05 level.

So significant different exist between the social empowerment of science- and arts-stream university women students through ICT confirming Hypothesis 2 i.e., a Significant difference exists between social empowerment of science and arts stream university women students through ICT.

Determination of the difference in educational empowerment of science- and Arts- University students' through ICT.

MEASURES / GROUPS	N	M	SD	SE_D	t	P
Science Educational	40	43.7	2.84	1.270	4.645	P< .01
Arts Educational	60	37.8	9.21			

Table 5: t- and p-value of the difference between mean scores in Educational Empowerment of Science- and Arts- Students' through ICT along with other relevant measures

Table 5 shows that the t-value between mean scores in educational empowerment of science- and arts- stream university women students' is 4.645 which is significant at less than the .01 level.

So significant difference exists between the educational empowerment of science- and arts-stream university women students' through ICT confirming Hypothesis 3 i.e., a Significant difference exists between educational empowerment of science and arts stream university women students' through ICT.

Conclusion

In this study, the personal, social, and educational empowerment of university women students through ICT was found. The study was done on science- and Arts- students'. The status of science- students in respect of personal and educational empowerment was shown sharply better than that of Arts- students. In the case of social empowerment, the difference is marginal.

A significant difference (<.01) is also seen between science- and Arts- students in respect of personal and educational students. In the case of social empowerment, the empowerment significant difference was also seen but the level was <.05

These findings support the status of personal, social, and educational empowerment of Science- and Arts- university students.

It can be concluded that Science- students' got too much more empowerment than their Arts- counterparts, in respect of Personal, Social, and Educational.

References

- Beena. (2015). Empowerment of rural women through ICT education- A case study (Doctoral dissertation, Banasthali University, 2015) from http://hdl.handle.net/10603/137787 retrieved on- 31.03.2022.
- Dinesh, MP. (2013). Role of Information Communication Technologies for Women empowerment: A Kerala experience. (Doctoral dissertation, University of Calicut).From https://hdl.handle.net/10603/215150 retrieved on 02.06.22.
- Fountain, JE. (2000). Constructing the information: Women, Information technology and design. Technology in society, 22, Pp. 45-62.
- Gupta, A. (2018). Making impact of Technology more powerful for women in Rural India. From https://www.shethepeople.tv/news/impact-technology-powerful-women-rural-India/ retrieved on 05.06.2022.
- Khan, YZ. (2015). ICT as a tool to empowering of Indian women. International journal of management research and social science, 2, Pp. 65-70.
- Khan, E. (2014). Women empowerment: Role of information communication technology(internet). International journal of scientific research, 3.
- Lyngkhoi, R. (2019). Information and communication technology ICT usage in changing lives of Tribal women's of hilly areas in Meghalaya. (Doctoral dissertation, North Eastern Hill University, 2019). From http://hdl.hdl.handle.net/10603/311630 retrieved on 28.06.2022.

- Mackey, A., & Petrucka, P. (2021). Technology as the key to women's empowerment: A scoping review. BMC Women's Health 21, 78(2021). From http://doi.org/10.1186/&12905-021-01225-4 retrieved on 22.05.2022.
- Mcleod, A. (2014). Community attitude and ICT intervention program for school girls. (Doctoral Dissertation, Monash University, Australia). From https://bridges.monash.edu/articles/thesis/community_attitudes_and_an_ICT_intervention_program_for_school_girl/4711663/1_ retrieved on 18.05.2022.
- Mookiah, M. & Prab, M. (2017). Role of information communication technology in women empowerment. Paper presented at the conference: Technology integration for educational empowerment of Women. Development of education, Alagappa University, Tamilnadu.
- Mohapatra, S. (2014). ICT and its impact on women: A study in two districts of Odisha. (Doctoral dissertation, University of Hyderabad). From http://hdl.handle.net/10603/314127 retrieved on 23.04.2022.
- Purushothman, A. (2011). Role of ICT in educational upliftment of women- Indian scenario. Proceedings of the 2011 World Congress on Information and communication technologies. Pp. 268-273.

DOI: 10.1109/WICT.2011.614190,10.1109/WICT.2011.6141256 retrieved on 28.07.2022.

- Rajput, K. (2021). Women empowerment through digital technology: International journal of scientific and research publications, 11(11). From http://dx.doi.org/10.29322/IJSRP.11.11.2021.p11959 retrieved on 05.04.2022.
- Subhramanian, C. (2012). Empowering women through information communication technology. International journal of recent scientific research, 3(5), Pp. 39-311.
- Voluntary Association for People Service. (2013). Enhancing women empowerment through information and communication technology: A Report. Government of India ministry of women and child development.